KISMET

Bright, Fresh, Vegetable-Loving Recipes

Sara Kramer and Sarah Hymanson

Photographs by Chris Bernabeo

KISMET

Clarkson Potter/Publishers
New York

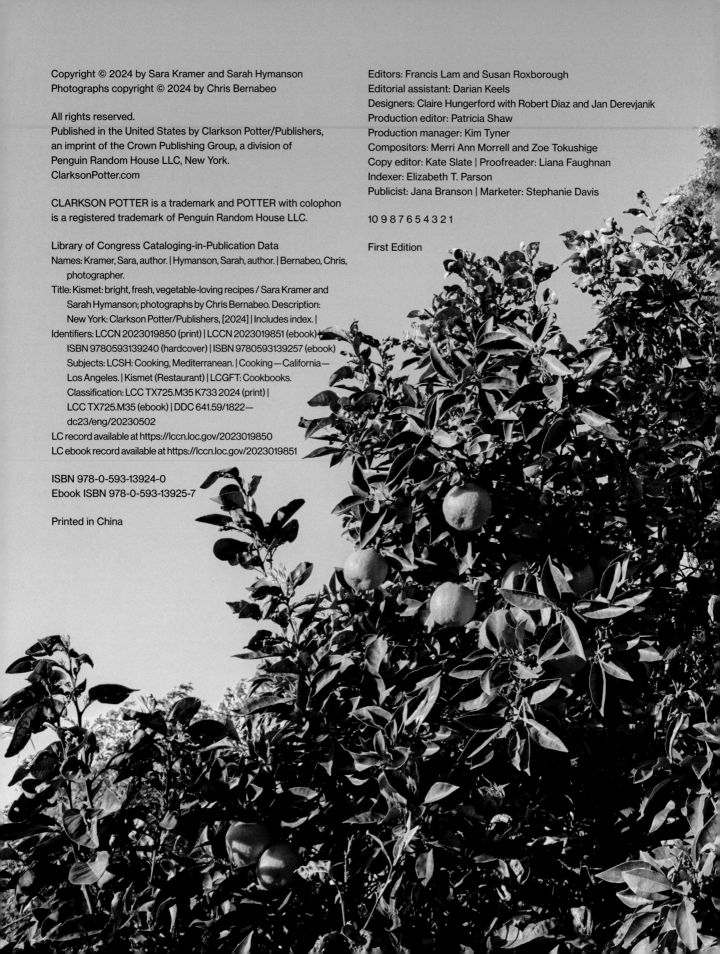

Published in the United States by Clarkson Potter/Publishers,
an imprint of the Crown Publishing Group, a division of
Penguin Random House LLC, New York.
ClarksonPotter.com

CLARKSON POTTER is a trademark and POTTER with colophon
is a registered trademark of Penguin Random House LLC.

Library of Congress Cataloging-in-Publication Data
Names: Kramer, Sara, author. | Hymanson, Sarah, author. | Bernabeo, Chris,
    photographer.
Title: Kismet: bright, fresh, vegetable-loving recipes / Sara Kramer and
    Sarah Hymanson; photographs by Chris Bernabeo. Description:
    New York: Clarkson Potter/Publishers, [2024] | Includes index. |
Identifiers: LCCN 2023019850 (print) | LCCN 2023019851 (ebook) |
    ISBN 9780593139240 (hardcover) | ISBN 9780593139257 (ebook)
Subjects: LCSH: Cooking, Mediterranean. | Cooking—California—
    Los Angeles. | Kismet (Restaurant) | LCGFT: Cookbooks.
Classification: LCC TX725.M35 K733 2024 (print) |
    LCC TX725.M35 (ebook) | DDC 641.59/1822—
    dc23/eng/20230502
LC record available at https://lccn.loc.gov/2023019850
LC ebook record available at https://lccn.loc.gov/2023019851

ISBN 978-0-593-13924-0
Ebook ISBN 978-0-593-13925-7

Printed in China

Editors: Francis Lam and Susan Roxborough
Editorial assistant: Darian Keels
Designers: Claire Hungerford with Robert Diaz and Jan Derevjanik
Production editor: Patricia Shaw
Production manager: Kim Tyner
Compositors: Merri Ann Morrell and Zoe Tokushige
Copy editor: Kate Slate | Proofreader: Liana Faughnan
Indexer: Elizabeth T. Parson
Publicist: Jana Branson | Marketer: Stephanie Davis

10 9 8 7 6 5 4 3 2 1

First Edition

Dedicated to our loving
and supportive parents,
Bruce, Debbie,
Eva, and Jerry

Contents

Salady 27

As Good Tomorrow 69 as It Is Today

Dips + Sauces 91

133 Main Event Veg

Recipe List

INTRODUCTION

Kismet means a little bit of magic, a feeling of fitting, a just rightness. Quite literally, it's fate. It's what we named our Los Angeles restaurants, but it's also so much more than that. It's our shared understanding of how we work and live in the world of food.

Concisely, here's what we're all about:

Untraditional food that understands tradition.

Craveability and comfort.

Source well and shop small (if you're able).

Lots of vegetables, a little meat.

Minimal waste (and minimal shame).

Never settle. But sometimes settle.

Food is better shared. So is cooking.

Things change. Work with what you've got.

Simple, but make it sparkle.

Always be learning.

Food is community.

One
Quick Thing

Yes, we're restaurant chefs. No, this isn't a restaurant book. Why? Because we want you to actually cook these recipes.

This book brings together family recipes, longstanding Kismet and Kismet Rotisserie menu classics, and newly developed ideas, all of which reflect our particular perspective on food. Our recipes have broad-ranging influences—Mediterranean and Middle Eastern being the most prominent—and illustrate our obsession with produce, a penchant for assertive and bright flavors, and our love of family-style meals where tables become tapestries of little dishes. Imagine swiping a piece of just-off-the-grill flatbread through ranchy labneh, biting through the flakes of phyllo surrounding a lemony chicken-and-pine-nut pie, then locking eyes with a lamb meatball, an array of spiced pickles and vegetables awaiting your fork's arrival. That's the vibe.

There are certainly dishes in this book from our restaurants, but they aren't exactly how we'd make them there, nor should they be. Restaurant cooking is different from cooking at home—that's true for us, too. We made every recipe in this book (several times!) in our no-dishwasher, no-frills home kitchens, adapting them for ease without sacrificing creativity or deliciousness.

These recipes are meant to keep you company for the long haul, from casual weeknight meals to party starters, from perfect potlucks to celebratory feasts. We hope these are dishes you keep coming back to, that these pages become stained with the pomegranate molasses smudges of meals past.

Sara Kramer
A Very Brief Bio

Born:
The Bronx, New York

Sign:
Aquarius Sun, Virgo Moon,
Aries Rising

First job:
scooping ice cream at
Temptations Café in
Nyack, New York

Was once a:
Broadway performer

Childhood pet:
you name it, we had them
all, including at least three
successive guinea pigs
named Dutchie

Ultimate comfort food:
buttery white rice with
fried eggs and cucumber-
tomato salad

Desert-island vegetable:
cucumbers

Forever ice-cream flavor:
strawberry

**When I'm not cooking
I'm probably:**
on the tennis court

Favorite movie:
The Fifth Element

Pet:
a doodle named Kevin

Why We Cook
How We Cook

Sara K: I have never seen empty space in my mother's kitchen cabinets. They are forever teeming with knotted baggies of seeds, unidentifiable jars of spices, cans of everyone's favorite pickles, too many jars of honey, enough rice to fill a kiddie pool, packets to make the Peruvian purple corn drink chicha morada, and many other mystery items. I've been known to do a little (unwelcome) tidying whenever I'm there, but it's always been worth braving the chaos to get a front-row seat at her stove.

Since moving to the United States at twenty-one, my mother has always channeled her sense of home through cooking. And thanks to her Jewish diasporic Peruvian-Israeli-Moroccan-Spanish background, she has as broad a relationship to flavor and ingredients as she has strong opinions in the kitchen. Being my mother's daughter, I stubbornly started stepping in to make my own dinners at age five. I can't even remember a time before I knew how to make malawach (page 224) or her mother's borekas (page 230).

My family aside, I've always been drawn to food from an ethical perspective and through an interest in ingredients themselves. And anyone who knows me can confirm that wherever my fascination lies, a very driven pursuit follows.

After spending my late teenage years belting out ABBA's best in *Mamma Mia!* on Broadway—a longer story for another time—I hard-pivoted, enrolling in a left-of-center culinary program at the Natural Gourmet Institute. From there, I interned at Blue Hill at Stone Barns, elbowing my way into a job cooking fancy farm-to-table food between their two locations for a couple of years. I then worked for a long stretch in Andrew Tarlow's restaurants in Brooklyn (Diner, Marlow and Sons, Roman's), all magical places.

Working in these and other restaurants allowed me to develop a sense of confidence and creative freedom in the kitchen. I began to feel a pull to cook food that felt a little closer to home, and luckily, I was offered a job as the opening chef of a restaurant called Glasserie, which allowed me to do just that.

Sarah H: In the days before smartphones, my dad carried around a thick stack of little yellow pieces of paper, torn from legal pads, tucked into the front pocket of his button-down shirt: a running list of places he wanted to eat. He was an early devotee of internet food forums and always had his ear to the ground, listening for anyone to say that they had tasted something delicious. While my mother did most of the cooking at home—which was heavy on legumes and rice—my obsession with food came from my father.

As a teenager in Chicago, I spent countless hours in restaurants with my friends: at a bustling Mexican breakfast spot, a late-night Taiwanese bubble tea café, a boundless Indian buffet. Taking me from one neighborhood to the next, restaurants helped me feel like I was part of a larger world.

At twenty, I got an internship at a restaurant in Brooklyn called (lowercase) applewood, a quaint but impressive neighborhood restaurant that was at the forefront of the farm-to-table movement. At applewood, I had my first tastes of Meyer lemon and soft-shell crab; I learned to butcher rabbits and fillet wreckfish. The physicality and intensity of the work suited me. I loved it.

On my days off, I ate delicious things from every corner of the city. I took the D train to Café Kashkar in Brighton Beach for dried-meat-and-pickle salad; the Number 7 train to the Golden Mall in Flushing for cold skin noodles from the original Xi'an Famous Foods; the F train to the now-closed Eagle Movie Theater in Jackson Heights, where they sold samosas at the concession stand.

After some years at applewood, I, too, worked at both Blue Hill and Blue Hill at Stone Barns, after which I joined the opening team of Mission Chinese Food in New York (and what a wild ride that was!).

Living in cities filled with such rich diasporic food traditions has hugely impacted who I am as a cook. I am always thinking about how ingredients or techniques fit into a larger web, ideas and traditions woven into an intricate lattice, one I am ever curious about. In many ways I'm like my dad,

showing up with a bunch of notepads, appreciative, and eager, more than anything, to learn.

Sara K: In 2013, I had just opened Glasserie in Greenpoint (Brooklyn)—my first head chef job—and I was drowning. Two or so months in, Sarah, who I'd briefly crossed paths with a few years earlier, came in for dinner (to size me up) (**SH:** perhaps) and mentioned she was looking for a new gig.

Sarah H: I was eating around, trying to figure out where I wanted to work, and was blown away by the food at Glasserie.

Sara K: After some heavy convincing, Sarah came on board as sous-chef, and our nascent partnership began to form. Turns out, our respective Blue Hill experiences were key, as were our Jewish-kid vegetarian years.

Sarah H: We found that we shared not just a love of salad but also an entrepreneurial spirit, the desire for a strong partnership, and a vision of something we wanted to build together.

Sara K: In 2014, the two of us decided to move from New York to LA, with restaurant-y stars in our eyes. Did we have any idea how to make this happen?

Sarah H: Nope. Did we know just how ambitious a plan this was?

Sara K: Sure didn't! We visited LA for maybe a week and, with very few connections, and even less money, we decided it felt worth the leap.

Sarah H: I'm honestly too pale for 360 days of sunshine, but I fell in love with LA regardless.

Sara K: I needed to leave New York or I never would, and need I mention the produce? It felt like a precipice moment, so we jumped.

Sarah Hymanson
A Very Brief Bio

Born:
Chicago, Illinois

Sign:
Gemini Sun, Taurus Moon,
Libra Rising

First job:
cleaning fish tanks
and selling dog food at
Parkview Pet Shop

Was once an:
acrobat

Childhood pet:
hedgehog

Ultimate comfort food:
rice with spicy sauce

Desert-island vegetable:
nutritious greens

Forever ice-cream flavor:
mint

**When I'm not cooking
I'm probably:**
collecting hobbies*

Favorite movie:
Desert Hearts

Pet:
I wish

Our first restaurant, Madcapra (later called Kismet Falafel), was born in 2015, with twelve stools at an L-shaped counter in LA's Grand Central Market. It was a falafel shop, but it was really more of a creative vegetarian café that happened to serve falafel. We prepped vats of pickles, rolled out and grilled flatbread to order, and served specials like green coriander soda alongside our menu of falafel wraps and salads. The little-falafel-shop-that-could hummed along for five good years, until we made the difficult decision to close it when the pandemic hit.

Our second act, Kismet, opened in 2017. The idea was to be a true neighborhood spot: our doors open daytime through dinner, the space either bright or appropriately dim, a song floating above the din of diners' voices, all in a welcoming room with colorful plates of undeniably delicious food. We envisioned a place where spices fragrantly adorn most dishes, where labneh is fermented in-house to serve alongside flaky, buttery malawach bread, where marinated feta is paired with an ever-rotating cast of fruits and vegetables.

We also knew we wanted to open a takeout-focused concept for everyday fare for all types of eaters. We quickly agreed that rotisserie chicken was the obvious choice, as something we both love and want to eat all the time, which brings us to our third act: Kismet Rotisserie. Arriving in January 2020, its opening couldn't have been timelier. Never in history had there been such a clear need for takeout, and we felt fortunate to be able to serve countless chickens, warm fluffy pitas, and marinated market vegetables to our community during that time.

And here we are now, several restaurants under our belts. This moment—and this book—is the culmination of nearly a decade of discovering and developing our shared identity. At the same time, it also marks something else: the next phase of Kismet, which somehow still feels like it's only beginning.

Our Favorite Everything

We're terrible at favorites (there's so much to love!), but there are a few things we couldn't live—or cook—without. These are our essential cooking tools and ingredients.

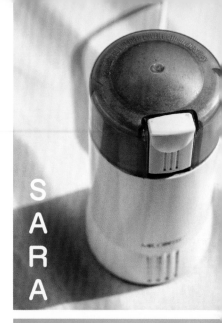

SPICE GRINDER

There's nothing wrong with using preground spices – especially in a pinch – but if you're really interested in building layers of flavor, this is a most useful tool. Toasting and grinding your own whole-seed spices, like cumin and coriander, will create a much more flavorful experience, and that's the whole point, isn't it? Plus, a spice grinder is useful for other things, too, like cracking sesame seeds. It's essentially a tiny food processor.

MICROPLANE

Extremely useful for grating citrus zest and garlic, a Microplane (specifically the classic zester/grater) breaks up the particles of an ingredient really, really finely, so the flavor and essence incorporate seamlessly into whatever you're making. It's great for little last touches, too, like finely grating cheese or macadamia nuts over a salad, or dusting chocolate over a dessert to make things feel a little fancy.

REVERSIBLE CAST-IRON GRIDDLE

It's often more convenient and practical to use a cast-iron griddle set over two burners on a stove rather than grill outside. Think of it as a plancha: You get deep caramelization without the smoke (or flare-ups) from a grill. That said, I also love putting the griddle directly on a fire (bring it camping!) to get a little bit of smoke without the intensity of a direct flame. I mostly use the flat side (though it's sometimes also nice to have the grill-pan option); it gets even color on whatever I'm cooking, whether that's toast or green beans or salmon.

SARA KRAMER'S FAVORITES

TOASTER OVEN

Maybe it's because my main oven is an over-qualified storage cabinet, but I cook everything in my toaster oven. To be specific, it's a Breville countertop oven that has more functions than anyone needs – but I love options! It's great for cooking for one or a small crowd. It cooks low, it cooks high, and it's very precise. It's great for an easy "reverse sear" on a steak or chop: Just set the temp to 180°F, cook the steak until the inside registers 120°F, let it rest, then quickly pop it into a hot cast-iron pan to sear. You can even dehydrate in it. Everyone who comes over and sees me using it is like, "I need one of these." Ya hear, Breville?

FRESH BAY LEAVES

I'll admit, dried bay leaves taste a little dusty, maybe because they've been gathering literal dust in a cabinet. Fresh bay leaves are way more vibrant; they add herbal warmth and roundness to our food. Pretty much any time we put something in a pot, it's got a bay leaf in it. For anyone who doubts the singular importance of bay leaves, buy some fresh ones, make two pots of beans side by side, and put a bay leaf in one of them. Then taste the difference and eat your words.

DAIRY (especially cultured dairy)

I have a deep love of dairy. In my fridge right now, I have cow's-milk yogurt, sheep's-milk yogurt, labneh, buttermilk, two or three types of butter, half-and-half, and at least four types of cheese. Cultured dairy – meaning it's gone through some kind of fermentation process – is one of the real miracles of the natural world. It's tangy, probiotic, and lasts for so long (in the fridge). There are very few things that I feel aren't made better by adding some kind of dairy component. Take the cucumber salad on page 29: a lovely salad on its own but truly stellar with the addition of rose water labneh.

CALZURO CLOGS

I can stand in these all day and actually feel pretty great come bedtime. They're made of rubber, which makes them feel cushioned and also means they're easy to clean – a huge win. Plus, they're just cool and come in every color. Mine are a matte green and, not to brag, I get compliments on them all the time.

APRON

Maybe it feels silly to wear an apron at home, but I highly recommend it. If I could time-machine back, I would have saved myself the anguish of ruining all my nice clothes every time oil has splattered on me while cooking. An apron doesn't need to be expensive – the point of it is to get dirty, after all. Plus, it's very handy to be able to tuck a kitchen towel into the string.

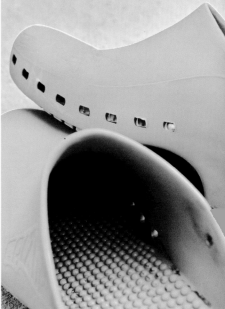

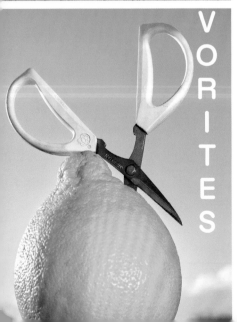

SARAH HYMANSON'S FAVORITES

FUN PANTS

Sure, hats and bandanas are fine, but fun pants are more my style. I take the time to dig through every pair of pants at the thrift store, looking for ones that are durable and, generally, cotton. I wear a lot of "working women" pants from the '90s. My favorite pair is a slightly tapered Liz Claiborne Sport number in a black-and-white check pattern oddly reminiscent of chefwear. Coming in at a close second are a pair of '60s flowery ones that might actually be pajamas.

SPRAY BOTTLE

I'm really into the spray bottle as an all-purpose tool. I like charred food plenty, but when cooking certain vegetables (like broccolini or other hardy greens) on a griddle or in a cast-iron pan, I like to cook them faster and more delicately by adding a spritz of water. The moisture slows down the char and speeds up the cooking by steaming the veg while searing: double action. Plus, it's hot in the kitchen — give your face a little refreshing Evian-mist-era spritz!

KITCHEN SCISSORS

Anyone who has eaten Korean barbecue won't question the usefulness of scissors. I'll cook a big pot of tangled greens and then run through the pot with scissors a few times to make them more manageable to eat. I also use scissors to cut up chicken — it's so easy. Be real casual, cut up the chicken on the roasting pan, and you are ready to go. No juices lost!

STEAMER

I keep a steamer on my stove at all times: It's a big, wide stainless steel pot with a steamer insert, which provides plenty of space for steam to evenly envelop vegetables. (I don't know why those small collapsible steamers were invented — everything is wrong with them.) It's great for carefully cooking vegetables, like squash or beets. Steaming maintains their integrity, holding on to flavor, nutrients, and shape. I often have steamed squash, rice, and a fried egg for breakfast.

RICE COOKER

I pride myself on my stovetop rice-cooking skills, but the reality is, at home I always use a rice cooker. I like that I can set it and forget it, and it's nice that it doesn't take up space on the stove. The one I use daily is extremely small — the smallest you can find, in fact — so it's . . . not for entertaining. I got it in 2004 (!) from an electronics store in Chicago, and it's still going strong.

SPICY STUFF

I need to be able to easily add spice to my food. At my house I have a million ground, dried, salted, preserved, and fermented chiles, of all kinds and various spice levels. I put chile on most things: dried chile flakes sprinkled on toast with nut butter, chile crisp on rice porridge, spicy Indian pickled ginger mixed into a marinade for chicken, chile vinegar tossed in with cooked greens . . . I could give up just about anything before chile.

BIG JARS

I love to ferment all kinds of things, especially garden overflow: cabbage, fennel, carrots, beans, turnip tops, you name it. Even if it's just adding a few tablespoons of the brine into a stew or a marinade, fermented foods impart an umami-filled, tangy layer to a dish. The reality is you can turn pretty much anything into a vessel for fermenting: I use various sizes of glass jars with air locks.

SMALL BAKING SHEETS

Cooking at home, I have my half-sheet pans (13 × 18 inches), but it's often a lot more manageable to use a quarter-sheet pan (9 × 13 inches) or even eighth-sheet pans (6½ × 9½ inches), so you're not dealing with large, hot pans if you don't have to. If I'm toasting some nuts or if I'm cooking a sweet potato or a piece of fish, it's nice to have small baking sheets that fit easily in my toaster oven. (I, too, swear by my Breville.)

MINI SPATULA

I cook a lot of saucy things, and a small silicone spatula has become my go-to tool. I like that it allows me to cleanly and gently move things around in a pot and really get in there, leaving little waste. Heating up leftovers in a nonstick pan? Check. Scrambling eggs? Check. Getting those last drops of sauce out of the blender? Check. Even though I have so many spoons, I often just use my little spatula. What can I say, I've always been partial to little things: little spoons, little pots, little bowls.

What
We Mean
When
We Say . . .

Here's a little cheat sheet for the ingredients and techniques we'll call for all the time.

SALT / Diamond Crystal kosher. Good size, good salinity level (the right amount of actual salt taste to volume), good price. If you're using Morton kosher salt, reduce the amount of salt called for by at least one-third. For more deep thoughts on salt, see Salt to Taste (page 155).

BLACK PEPPER / We want you to grind whole peppercorns yourself, in a pepper grinder or a spice grinder. Use preground only in a pinch.

NEUTRAL OIL / Flavorless, high-temperature oil such as canola, sunflower, safflower, avocado, or grapeseed, especially for searing and frying.

OLIVE OIL / Extra-virgin only. "Pure" is not it.

BUTTER / Unsalted.

CHICKEN STOCK / Made at home using more bones than you think, and nothing else—just bones. We're talking a pot of bones, roasted or not, covered in water, brought up to a boil and then simmered for no fewer than 4 hours, then strained. That's the ticket. A good alternative is to purchase stock from a shop that makes it, like a butcher shop or local grocery store. The boxed varieties are thin and filled with flavorings and vegetables, and they really pale in comparison. The most important detail is that it should have no salt.

BAY LEAVES / Fresh. The flavor of dried bay leaves just can't compete.

GROUND SPICES / Whole spices, ground at home. You can buy preground spices, for sure, but grinding whole spices yourself will yield more vibrant flavor. To lighten the load of grinding spices every time you need to use them, you can grind more than you need for a single recipe, then store them in an airtight container, and use them for a few weeks.

TOASTED NUTS / Low and slow: 275°F for 30 to 40 minutes. This gets them toasted evenly all the way through, rather than dark on the outside, crudo in the middle.

GRATED GARLIC / On a Microplane, to incorporate seamlessly into whatever you're cooking.

TOSSING A SALAD / With your hands, so you don't bruise the leaves with tongs. Be as gentle as possible, lifting from the bottom, with wide-set fingers.

Salady

As far as we're concerned, pretty much anything can be a salad. Little Gem lettuce with toasted pistachios? Obviously. But don't count out persimmons with capers, cold shrimp with apples, or poached chicken with tomatoes. Perhaps they're not traditional salads, but they are salady: cold or room-temp dishes that want to be eaten right away, always involving a fruit or vegetable or several, with a sharp hit of acid. Salady is all about living that peak produce life.

Can't-Take-It-Off-the-Menu Cucumber Salad

This salad's enduring popularity on the Kismet menu proves, year after year, that cucumbers are universally loved. There are few fruits that won't make a nice sidekick to bright, crisp cucumbers. If cherries aren't in season, celebrate the fruit of the moment: We've cycled through mandarin oranges, melons, mulberries, and persimmons. As for rose water labneh, it's the sauce you never knew you needed.

Get Ahead
Make the parsley seed za'atar and rose water labneh up to 3 days ahead.

Parsley Seed Za'atar
4 teaspoons sesame seeds
1 tablespoon dried rose petals, crumbled between your fingers[1]
1 teaspoon sumac
½ teaspoon parsley seeds[2]
⅛ teaspoon kosher salt

Rose Water Labneh
1 cup labneh, store-bought or homemade (page 98)
Grated zest of ¼ lemon
1 teaspoon rose water
½ garlic clove, grated on a Microplane
¼ teaspoon kosher salt
Pinch of ground black pepper

Salad
2 tablespoons lemon juice (about 1 lemon)
1 tablespoon olive oil
2 teaspoons kosher salt
5 Persian (mini) cucumbers, shaved lengthwise on a mandoline into ⅛-inch-thick slabs[3]
2 cups cherries, pitted and halved
¼ cup chervil, mint, or parsley leaves

1   **Make the parsley seed za'atar:** Preheat the oven to 300°F.

2   Spread the sesame seeds on a small baking sheet and toast for 30 minutes, stirring occasionally. Remove from the oven and let cool. Lightly grind in a spice grinder or mortar and pestle to a sandy texture (not a fine powder).

3   In a small bowl, stir together the ground sesame seeds, dried rose petals, sumac, parsley seeds, and salt. Set aside.

4   **Prepare the rose water labneh:** In a small bowl, combine the labneh, lemon zest, rose water, grated garlic, salt, and black pepper and stir to distribute the ingredients thoroughly. Store in the fridge until ready to use.

5   **Assemble the salad:** In a medium bowl, whisk together the lemon juice, olive oil, and salt. Add the shaved cucumbers to the bowl and toss to coat.

6   Spread the rose water labneh on the bottom of a serving dish or bowl. Using your hands, arrange the cucumber slices into loose curls and set on top of the labneh.

7   Top with the cherries, followed by the za'atar and chervil.

1
Dried rose petals can be a little leathery. Stick them in a very low oven (200°F or less) for 10 to 15 minutes for a little extra drying. Once they're completely cool, they should be crumbly.

2
We source our parsley seeds from garden supply stores — may we recommend the internet? Celery seed will make a fine sub, for something you can snag from a supermarket.

3
Shaving on a mandoline is a little intimidating, especially when your palm ends up kissing the blade toward the end. In the name of safety, ditch the last slice. For an even more cautious approach, you can cut the cucumbers on a bias into 1½-inch pieces instead of shaving.

Little Gems with Grape-Leaf Vinaigrette

This all-seasons salad has become a fixture on the Kismet menu, and it's all thanks to the grape-leaf vinaigrette. Dried and powdered grape leaves lend a distinct (and delicious) briny herbaceousness to an otherwise simple white wine vinaigrette. Making that grape-leaf powder might seem intimidating, but it's actually a very simple process (and you can make it ages in advance). Omit it, and the dish will still be lovely, but its inclusion helps this salad hit the highest of high notes.

> **Get Ahead**
> Doing the work of prepping the grape-leaf powder and, subsequently, the dressing days or weeks ahead will make this salad feel effortless.

Grape-Leaf Vinaigrette

1 teaspoon Grape-Leaf Powder
  (recipe follows)
3 tablespoons olive oil
3 tablespoons white wine vinegar
1 teaspoon honey
1 teaspoon kosher salt

Salad

½ cup pistachios
¼ cup kosher salt
2 cups sugar snap peas, trimmed
  (6 to 8 ounces)[1]
2 heads Little Gem lettuce,[2]
  leaves separated
¾ cup mint leaves

1 **Make the grape-leaf vinaigrette:** In a small bowl, whisk together the grape-leaf powder, olive oil, white wine vinegar, honey, and salt. Set aside.

2 Preheat the oven to 275°F.

3 **Prep the salad:** Spread the pistachios on a baking sheet and bake until lightly browned, 30 to 40 minutes. Let cool, then roughly chop.

4 Meanwhile, in a medium pot, bring 3 cups water and the salt to a boil. Blanch the sugar snap peas for 1 to 2 minutes. Using a slotted spoon or spider, remove the peas and lay them flat on a baking sheet to cool. Slice the peas into ¼" rounds or in half on a bias.

5 **Assemble the salad:** In a large bowl, combine the snap peas, pistachios, and lettuce leaves. Toss the salad with the vinaigrette. Add the mint leaves, toss lightly, and serve.

Grape-Leaf Powder

MAKES 1 TABLESPOON

Grape-Leaf Powder

8 preserved grape leaves[3]

1 Preheat the oven to 250°F. Set a wire rack inside a baking sheet.

2 Lay the grape leaves flat on the wire rack. Place in the oven for about 25 minutes, or until fully dried. Remove from the oven and let cool to room temperature.

3 Grind the leaves in a spice grinder and then sift through a fine-mesh sieve to a powder. (Toss any excess larger bits.)

1
It's a nice touch to string your snap peas. Use a paring knife to clip the pointy top of the pea, not cutting all the way through, then pull the string of the flat side down the body of the pea. Shaved fennel is a solid sub if snap peas aren't in season.

2
Little Gems, if you're not familiar, are a small, sweet, and very crisp romaine-adjacent lettuce. No gems handy? Any snappy lettuce, romaine included, will do.

3
These are your standard variety canned grape leaves – the kind you'd buy for dolma.

Spicy Watermelon + Feta Salad

Watermelon is so wonderful on its own that we almost hate suggesting you serve it any way other than straight-up. That said, it's also great grilled (yes, grilled), ceviche-d, or cubed in a salad, such as here. Watermelon and feta are a pretty classic combo, and classics die hard. We're adding to the canon, spicing up the duo with fresh chile and cardamom. Grill a few sausages and some ears of corn and you're all set with a speedy summer feast.

⅓ cup olive oil

1 teaspoon freshly ground black pepper

1 teaspoon ground cardamom

½ red onion, thinly sliced

1 red Fresno chile,[1] thinly sliced into rounds

2 tablespoons lemon juice (about 1 lemon)

2 teaspoons kosher salt

8 cups cubed watermelon
(about ½ large watermelon)

7 ounces feta cheese, broken into
bite-size chunks

1 cup basil leaves (torn, if large)

1 In a small saucepan, combine the olive oil, black pepper, and cardamom and gently warm over medium-low heat, swirling, for 2 to 3 minutes, to let the spices bloom.

2 In a small bowl, combine the sliced onion, chile, lemon juice, and salt. Toss together. Pour the warm oil over the seasoned onions and chiles and toss to combine.

3 Arrange the watermelon on a large platter.

4 Pour the marinated onions and chiles over the watermelon and, using your hands or a large spoon, gently toss to coat. Top with the feta and basil and serve.

---

[1] Chiles can vary widely in heat level. Unless you're into that hot hot heat, to make sure you're not overwhelming your salad with too much spice, you should taste the chile first to help you decide if you want to use the whole thing. (Taste from the middle, as the tip of the chile is always less spicy.)

Butter Lettuce with Avocado + Sweet Corn

Butter lettuce is unparalleled in the lettuce kingdom for its supple, sweet appeal. We might even go out on a limb and call it seductive—if you're into that sort of thing—and, well, we are! It's just a sexy lettuce! Here we're giving it some worthy partners with summer corn, rich crème fraîche dressing, and ripe avocado. This salad is a textural pleasure palace, be warned.

Grilled Corn
2 ears corn, husked
1 teaspoon olive oil
¼ teaspoon kosher salt

Dressing
¾ cup crème fraîche
2 tablespoons olive oil
1 teaspoon kosher salt
Grated zest of ½ lemon
3 tablespoons lemon juice
    (about 1½ lemons)

Salad
2 heads butter lettuce,
    leaves separated
1 shallot, thinly sliced into rounds
1 avocado, thinly sliced
2 teaspoons Urfa pepper[1]
½ cup basil leaves

1 **Grill the corn:** Preheat a grill to high heat.

2 Using your hands, coat the corn with the olive oil and sprinkle evenly with the salt.

3 Grill over high heat, turning on all sides until visibly (but not overly) charred, about 10 minutes. Let cool to room temperature.

4 One at a time, hold each ear of corn vertically in a large bowl and cut the kernels from the cobs down into the bowl.

5 **Make the dressing:** In a small bowl, combine the crème fraîche, olive oil, salt, lemon zest, and lemon juice and whisk to combine.[2]

6 **Assemble the salad:** In a large bowl, toss the butter lettuce with the sliced shallot and dressing to coat. Transfer the dressed lettuce to a serving dish. Top with the corn and the avocado slices. Sprinkle the Urfa pepper over the top and finish with the basil.

1
If you can't get your hands on Urfa pepper (or *biber,* Turkish for "pepper"), freshly cracked black pepper can work here, but Urfa embodies a genuinely special combination of flavors. It's only mildly spicy, letting its smoky, sweet, and dried fruit–like qualities shine. It's worth seeking out at your local specialty store, or buy it online from Kalustyan's.

2
This dressing is going to feel thick, and that's what we're going for.

Summer's Finest Salad

Tomatoes and stone fruit: Name a more iconic duo. Particularly at the peak of summer, you can't do much better than the marriage of two (or three) perfect fruits in this simple stunner of a salad. We've made more complex versions in the past with olives and pine nuts and different herbs, but we've found that less here is most certainly more.

3 tablespoons minced shallot
(about 1 shallot)

1 tablespoon orange marmalade

3 tablespoons white wine vinegar

3 tablespoons olive oil

1½ teaspoons kosher salt

¼ teaspoon ground turmeric

¼ teaspoon freshly ground black pepper

3 medium tomatoes

3 stone fruits, such as nectarines or peaches, pitted

1 In a medium bowl, combine the shallots, orange marmalade, vinegar, olive oil, salt, turmeric, and black pepper. Whisk to combine and set aside.

2 Cut the tomatoes and stone fruit into large bite-size pieces.

3 Just before serving, add the tomatoes and fruit to the bowl with the vinaigrette and toss gently.

Miso-Poppy Dressing: An Origin Story

As a teen in the late '90s, I did a ton of babysitting. I don't remember the kids much at all, but I do remember what they would eat. One family often ordered this particular salad from a classically "American" restaurant called John's Place. It was a chopped salad with apples, pecans, and onion-poppy dressing. I had never had poppy seed dressing, and I was so into it.

When we opened Kismet Rotisserie, we wanted the menu to hint at our '90s adolescence. And though not quite on the level of *NOW That's What I Call Music* and "flares," poppy seed dressing definitely made its mark. The popularity of this dressing in my childhood is a bit of a mystery; it was a throwback to the '50s and somehow found its way into the "health food" category despite being full of sugar. Alongside the equally popular raspberry vinaigrette, it seemed to be everywhere.

As we were developing the Rotisserie menu, a poppy seed dressing felt like just the thing to make a version of a wedge salad feel like . . . us. We wanted a creamy white dressing, à la ranch or blue cheese, but lighter—something you could eat every day. We needed it to stay emulsified but wanted it to be vegan (i.e., eggless), which is why we turned to aquafaba, the cooking liquid left over from cooking chickpeas (of which we had plenty). We wanted it to be less sweet, so we used honey instead of sugar and added miso to boost the umami, rounding out the flavors. The resulting dressing became a Rotisserie staple that, hundreds of gallons later, still takes me back.

—Sarah Hymanson

Wedge Salad with Miso-Poppy Dressing

Not to be outshined by the roast chicken, this simple salad is the star of the show at Kismet Rotisserie. There's a reason we opted to have it take center stage: Iceberg's got style. Beloved across genres, from greasy burger topper to fancy steak house side dish, she's an icon among lettuces. Really though, how does iceberg do it? It never gets soggy—not even under a blanket of creamy, umami-rich, vegan (!) miso-poppy dressing. The crunch just won't quit, and neither will our love for it.

Get Ahead

The dressing will hold well for several days in the fridge, but because of the fresh lemon juice, it does change a little over time. It tastes its absolute best on day one, an hour or two after it's made.

Miso-Poppy Dressing

¼ cup white miso
1 tablespoon plus 1 teaspoon honey
1 teaspoon yellow mustard
1 teaspoon onion powder
1 tablespoon kosher salt
⅓ cup distilled white vinegar
Grated zest of ½ lemon
2 tablespoons lemon juice
    (about 1 lemon)
⅓ cup aquafaba,[1] from 1 (15-ounce)
    can chickpeas[2]
1 cup neutral oil, such as canola or sunflower
1½ teaspoons poppy seeds

Salad

1 head iceberg lettuce, cut into 4 wedges
6 to 8 radishes, any variety,
    thinly sliced on a mandoline
2 scallions, thinly sliced into rounds
1 cup parsley leaves

1 **Make the miso-poppy dressing:** In a blender, combine the miso, honey, mustard, onion powder, salt, vinegar, lemon zest, lemon juice, and aquafaba. Blend on medium-high speed for 10 seconds and, while the blender is still running, stream in the oil, pouring slowly to emulsify.

2 Once the oil is completely incorporated, add the poppy seeds and blend for just a second or two to distribute, then turn off the blender immediately. Store in the fridge until ready to use.[3]

3 **Assemble the salad:** Place the wedges of iceberg on a platter (or plate individually). Spoon a generous amount of the dressing over the wedges. Scatter the radishes, scallions, and parsley over the top.

[1]
Aquafaba is the viscous liquid in a can of chickpeas, which works miraculously well as an emulsifying agent. (It acts the same way as an egg, so if you don't have chickpea liquid handy, feel free to use one egg yolk instead.)

[2]
Just to be clear, you're not using the chickpeas here, just the liquid. Might we suggest making this on the same day you make the Moroccan-Spiced Carrots (page 142)?

[3]
This recipe may yield just a little too much dressing – then again, when it comes to a wedge, is there ever too much dressing? But a little extra for future salads is always welcome.

The Many Faces of Feta

Creamy, salty, fatty, and forever flexible, marinated feta goes with anything and everything. We've riffed on it no fewer than a hundred ways over the years, so choosing just a few iterations was a task. Happily, we've landed here: a selection of our favorites. Whether you pair the feta with spice-roasted tomatoes (page 47) or grilled endive (page 51), any of these makes a perfect starter. You'll look like you've really got it together if you have a plate of marinated feta waiting next to some good bread when friends come over.

Our Marinated Feta

No matter the pairing, our feta always starts with an infused oil. The flavors in this oil were inspired by a particular marinated goat cheese from an Australian producer, Meredith Dairy. Aromatic with toasty garlic, lemon zest, and black pepper, when paired with creamy cheese, this is about as satisfying as it gets. You can make the feta oil weeks ahead and keep it in the fridge. We even recommend doubling or tripling the batch so you have it hanging around for whenever feta calls. It's also handy to have around for other uses, like dressing salads and marinating vegetables.

Get Ahead

The marinated feta holds up to 1 week in the fridge. Let it come to room temperature at least an hour before serving — oil solidifies when it's cold, and that's not so pleasant on the palate.

Infused Oil[1]
¼ cup olive oil
Grated zest of 1 lemon
½ garlic clove, grated on a Microplane
1 bay leaf
1 teaspoon coriander seeds
½ teaspoon black peppercorns

Feta
1 (7-ounce) package feta, such as Valbreso

1 **Infuse the oil:** In a small saucepan, combine the olive oil, lemon zest, garlic, bay leaf, coriander, and peppercorns. Heat gently[2] over very low heat for 30 minutes to infuse, stirring occasionally to break up any clumps.

2 Strain the oil into a small container and discard the solids. Let the oil cool to room temperature.

3 **Marinate the feta:** In a small bowl, crumble the feta into large chunks. Cover the feta with the aromatic oil and let marinate for at least 30 minutes.

4 Serve immediately or refrigerate for up to 1 week.

[1]
It's nice to use whole spices to infuse the feta oil and then strain them out. This way, you'll get a clear end result, as opposed to one flecked with aromatics — a little trick to keep things pretty.

[2]
You want to avoid caramelization on the garlic, so if you need to turn the heat on and off to keep it from browning, do it.

Marinated Feta with Dates + Rose Water Onions

Sweet and salty: the ultimate collab. Maybe the most crowd-pleasing feta friend of all, dates are decadent and deeply comforting. If you've been scared of rose water in the past, these onions might just turn your potpourri-fueled bias right around.

Get Ahead
After pulling the shaved onions from their ice bath, you can stash them in the fridge until ready to dress.

½ white onion or 4 cipollini onions, peeled and thinly shaved on a mandoline
3 tablespoons olive oil
2 bay leaves
1 cup dates,[1] pitted and halved
2 tablespoons date molasses[2]
4 teaspoons plus 2 tablespoons white wine vinegar
1 teaspoon rose water
¼ teaspoon kosher salt
Our Marinated Feta (page 43)
6 perilla, shiso, or mint leaves, torn

1   Soak the shaved onions in a bowl of ice water for 30 minutes.

2   Meanwhile, in a small saucepan, combine the olive oil and bay leaves and heat over medium-low heat until fragrant, 3 to 5 minutes, being careful not to burn the bay leaves.

3   Place the dates in a small heatproof bowl and pour the hot bay oil over them. Toss gently to coat and let cool to room temperature. Discard the bay leaves.

4   In a small bowl, combine the date molasses and 4 teaspoons of the vinegar and whisk into a smooth syrup. Pour into the bowl with the warm dates.

5   When ready to serve, remove the onions from the ice water, shake off the residual water, and place in a small dry bowl.[3] Add the remaining 2 tablespoons vinegar, the rose water, and salt and toss.

6   Transfer the marinated feta to a serving plate and spoon the dates in syrup over it. Top with the prepared onions and mint leaves.

[1] If you have access to farmers' market dates as we do here in LA, get any variety they've got — they're all great. If buying at a supermarket, we recommend Medjool. If the dates are huge, cut them in quarters.

[2] Date molasses isn't too difficult to find these days, and it's even simpler to order online, but if you don't have it on hand, honey's a fine substitute.

[3] You don't want to dress your onions too early. We're looking for lively, not limp!

Marinated Feta with Spice-Roasted Tomatoes + Grapefruit

Tomatoes and grapefruit may appear to be seasonally inappropriate bedfellows, but here in LA, we're blessed with the bounty of both throughout the winter months. The combination is nothing short of Shakespearean: a love match for the ages.

Get Ahead

The roasted tomatoes hold well in the fridge for up to 4 days.

Spice-Roasted Tomatoes

2 cups cherry tomatoes, halved
⅓ cup olive oil
1½ teaspoons Aleppo pepper
1 teaspoon kosher salt
1 teaspoon ground coriander
½ teaspoon freshly ground black pepper
¼ teaspoon ground fennel
¼ teaspoon ground cloves
1 teaspoon red wine vinegar
2 teaspoons pomegranate molasses

Assembly

1 grapefruit
Our Marinated Feta (page 43)
¼ cup tarragon leaves[1]

1 **Roast the tomatoes:** Preheat the oven to 400°F.

2 In a small bowl, combine the cherry tomatoes, olive oil, Aleppo pepper, salt, coriander, black pepper, fennel, and cloves and toss to coat. Transfer to a small ovenproof dish, ideally in a single layer, and roast, stirring as needed to avoid burning, until the tomatoes are blistered but maintain some structure, 15 to 20 minutes.

3 Let the tomatoes cool to room temperature, then toss to coat in the spices and oil from the bottom of the pan—you want all of the juices. Transfer to a small bowl, add the vinegar and pomegranate molasses, and mix to combine.

4 **Supreme the grapefruit:** Cut the peel and white pith away from the grapefruit with a sharp knife, then cut segments away from between the membranes around the core. Squeeze the juice from the core into the bowl with the segments and discard the squeezed-out bits.[2]

5 Spoon the marinated feta onto a serving dish. Arrange the roasted tomatoes (and any accumulated juices) and the grapefruit segments over the feta, and top with the tarragon.

[1] We love using huacatay here (aka black mint, the very aromatic leaves of a Peruvian marigold) in place of tarragon. If you're able to grow some, it's definitely worth adding to your garden.

[2] You can spoon a little of the juice along with the segments to the final dish, or enjoy a little invigorating behind-the-scenes shot of grapefruit juice.

Marinated Feta with Roasted Squash + Anchovy-Caramelized Onions

Anchovies are divisive, but real talk, they're divine. If you don't love them, as much as we'd love to convince you otherwise, it's 100 percent fine to leave them out. You're only missing out on one of the world's best salty-savory little sneak attacks, but it's okay! We trust your judgment.

Get Ahead

The caramelized onions hold like a dream in the fridge for up to 1 week. And if you were to decide to make extra, they're perfect to spread on a piece of toast under a fried egg.

1 small butternut squash, peeled, halved lengthwise, seeded, and cut into 1-inch pieces
1 tablespoon olive oil
1 teaspoon kosher salt

Anchovy-Caramelized Onions
2 yellow onions, cut into ½-inch pieces
¼ cup olive oil
1½ teaspoons kosher salt
¼ teaspoon freshly ground black pepper
1 sprig rosemary
1 tablespoon apple cider vinegar
2 teaspoons chopped oil-packed anchovies (about 6 fillets)

Assembly
1 small crisp apple, such as Granny Smith or Honeycrisp, thinly sliced
1 tablespoon lemon juice (about ½ lemon)
¼ cup parsley leaves
Our Marinated Feta (page 43)

1 Preheat the oven to 425°F.

2 In a medium bowl, coat the butternut squash pieces in the olive oil and sprinkle with the salt. Spread into one even layer on a baking sheet and roast for 30 minutes, flipping halfway through.

3 **Caramelize the onions:** In a medium saucepan, combine the onions, olive oil, salt, black pepper, and rosemary. Cook over low heat, stirring often and scraping up any stuck bits, until well caramelized, about 40 minutes.[1]

4 Remove and discard the rosemary stem. Add the vinegar, scraping up any stuck bits, and cook down until evaporated, about 1 minute. Remove from the heat and stir in the anchovies.

5 **To assemble:** In a small bowl, toss the apple slices with the lemon juice and parsley.

6 Lay the roasted squash pieces on a plate, and dot with spoonfuls of the caramelized onions in the spaces between. Spoon the marinated feta into the open spaces, and top the whole thing with the apple-parsley salad.

[1]
The onions should look medium brown and be soft and jammy, not at all chewy. Keep them from burning by pouring a little water down the sides of the pan to help pull the sticky browned bits that accumulate back into the onions. The water will cook out, so don't you worry 'bout a thing.

Marinated Feta with Grilled Endive + Chamomile Honey

My mom could eat the same thing every day. It's not that she doesn't like trying new foods; she does. She just doesn't seek them out, happy to eat the things she likes often. One of those things is Belgian endive. Kind of an unusual favorite food, I know, but she loves bitter flavors. Throughout my childhood, she would make herself a big endive salad, dressed simply with olive oil and red wine vinegar, covered by a heavy snowfall of Kraft Parmesan. She would eat straight from a big metal mixing bowl, and every year or so I'd try a bite. When I was really little, I didn't care for it but, gradually over the span of the next ten years, I came around. It was cheesy, tangy, and, as it turns out, I, too, love bitter flavors.

In this recipe, the endive is transformed into something juicy and sweet, balancing out any bitterness: a compromise I think both my mother and my childhood self would enjoy. —Sarah Hymanson

> **Get Ahead**
> Chamomile honey holds forever. Make it whenever you like!

Chamomile Honey
2 tablespoons honey
½ teaspoon dried chamomile[1]
½ teaspoon ground caraway
1½ teaspoons white wine vinegar

Grilled Endive
2 Belgian endives, halved lengthwise, keeping the root end intact
1 tablespoon neutral oil, such as canola
1 teaspoon kosher salt

Our Marinated Feta (page 43)
¼ teaspoon thyme leaves (optional)

1 **Make the chamomile honey:** In a small pot, combine the honey, chamomile, caraway, vinegar, and 1½ teaspoons water. Cook over low heat for 5 to 8 minutes.[2] Remove from the heat and let cool to room temperature.

2 **Grill the endives:** Preheat a grill to medium heat.[3]

3 In a small bowl, toss the endive halves with the oil and salt. Grill over a medium flame, flipping as needed, until lightly charred and the core begins to feel tender, 10 to 12 minutes. Remove from the grill and transfer to a serving plate.

4 Add the feta to the serving plate. Pour the infused honey over the feta and endive, sprinkle with thyme (if using), and serve.

---

[1] If you don't have access to loose dried chamomile, empty the contents of a chamomile tea bag. Just be sure it isn't a blend.

[2] You're looking to cook the liquid out to get back to the consistency of honey; it's not a heavy reduction.

[3] If you don't have a grill, you can broil the endives in the oven or pan-roast them in a cast-iron skillet.

Summer Spoon Salad

SERVES 4

"Spoon salad" may not be a ubiquitous term, but it does feel like it fits when the best tool for eating a salad is, in fact, a spoon. This spoon salad is a riff on a classic Middle Eastern tomato and cucumber salad, replacing the tomatoes with melon and adding avocado because, well, California. We mix the avo in at the end to keep it from completely breaking down, but a light toss will lend a satisfying, natural creaminess to the dressing.

2 cups diced seeded green melon
(about ½ melon), such as honeydew
2 cups diced Persian (mini) cucumbers
(3 or 4 cucumbers)
2 tablespoons finely chopped white onion
2 teaspoons kosher salt
¼ cup olive oil
¼ cup lemon juice (about 2 lemons)
⅛ teaspoon freshly ground black pepper
1 avocado, diced
½ cup basil leaves, torn, if large
¼ cup dill leaves

1   In a large bowl, combine the diced melon, cucumbers, and onion.

2   Add the salt, olive oil, lemon juice, and black pepper and toss together to coat.

3   Add the diced avocado, basil, and dill and lightly toss before serving.

A Lifelong Love of Salad Juice

Even if you're not familiar with the term (and why should you be?), you've surely encountered salad juice: the pool of liquid at the bottom of a (typically nonleafy) salad, where the dressing has mingled with the juices of the veg. It just might be the best thing about certain types of salads. Our Summer Spoon Salad (opposite) is a particularly prime example of a salad-juice salad.

In my house growing up, we'd eat a salad similar to this one at least twice a week. There were always chopped tomatoes and cucumbers, then the occasional guest-starring onion, pepper, or avocado. Like the ongoing fight between my sister and me over who got to eat the top of the Friday night apple cake (the most coveted part), salad juice was highly sought after. I have to imagine you've found yourself lapping up the liquid at the bottom of a good salad at least once in your life.

Working in fine-dining kitchens as an adult, I encountered a thing called "tomato water." If you've never seen it, tomato water is the blush-tinted, clear liquid drawn from a fresh tomato, often seasoned with herbs or spices— and there was a time when it had a real moment across restaurant menus. Suddenly, it was being used as the pristine base of anything from cocktails to exceptionally light clam chowder, and in the case of something like a "tomato-water gazpacho," I realized it was just, you guessed it, fancy salad juice. Fine dining had caught up with my cherished childhood obsession, drinking the contents of the bottom of the salad bowl.

—Sara Kramer

A Salty-Sweet Persimmon Salad

Persimmons are a cool-weather sweet treat. They're a fine friend for a cheese board and make a nice addition to morning granola, but they really shine in savory salads. We'd even say that we prefer—in fact, much prefer—them in nonsweet settings. They're quite mellow, with not a drop of acid, so a sharp vinaigrette brings a whole lot of necessary zing to the persimmon party. Here, the tang's coming in the form of a simple shallot vinaigrette, dressed up with salty, herbal capers and crunchy rosemary.

¼ cup olive oil

3 tablespoons capers, drained (or rinsed, if salt-packed)

2 tablespoons rosemary leaves

2 tablespoons finely minced shallot (about ½ shallot)

3 tablespoons lemon juice (about 1½ lemons)

1 teaspoon kosher salt

4 Fuyu persimmons,[1] peeled and shaved to ⅛ inch to ¼ inch thick on a mandoline

Freshly ground black pepper

1 Line a dish with paper towels. Place a fine-mesh sieve over a medium bowl. In a small skillet, combine the olive oil, capers, and rosemary and cook over medium heat, swirling often, until the capers and rosemary are crunchy, about 5 minutes.

2 Pour the hot oil through the prepared sieve into the bowl, catching the capers and rosemary. Set the capers and rosemary aside on the paper towels.

3 Once the oil has cooled to room temperature, stir in the shallot, lemon juice, and salt.

4 When ready to serve, lay the persimmons flat on a serving platter and spoon the lemon dressing over top. Sprinkle with the capers, rosemary, and douse with a few healthy cracks of freshly ground black pepper.

[1] Word to the wise: Beware the Hachiya persimmon. They're the more conical variety, and an underripe one (any stage before complete mush) is an exceptionally unpleasant lesson in astringence. Here you want only firm Fuyu persimmons, the squatter variety. The skin is edible – leave it on if you like – but we like them skinless.

Fancy Frisée Salad

It might be a bit of a hunt to get your hands on some passion fruits, but if you've never sought out a fresh one, you're going to be thrilled by what you find. They're floral, intoxicating, and look like wrinkly little alien eggs, plus they bring a hint of tropical flair to this otherwise understated salad.

Vinaigrette

2 tablespoons passion fruit pulp, with
    seeds (2 or 3 passion fruits)[1]
2 teaspoons minced shallot
    (about ½ shallot)
¼ teaspoon thyme leaves
2 tablespoons white wine vinegar
½ teaspoon kosher salt
1½ teaspoons honey
3 tablespoons olive oil
½ teaspoon Marash chile flakes[2]

Salad

1 golden beet, scrubbed and
    thinly sliced on a mandoline[3]
1 large or 2 small heads frisée, trimmed
    from the root, separated into pieces

1 **Make the vinaigrette:** In a small bowl, combine the passion fruit pulp and shallot and whisk to break up any stuck bits. Add the thyme, vinegar, salt, honey, olive oil, and Marash chile and whisk to combine.

2 **Assemble the salad:** In a medium bowl, dress the shaved beets with the vinaigrette and let sit for a minute or two to soften.

3 Add the frisée and toss to coat. Serve right away.

1
Alternatively, you can use frozen passion fruit puree (thawed, obviously), but it lacks a little bit of the intensity of the fresh fruit, so you might want to liven it up with a teaspoon of lemon juice.

2
Marash chile is nice here because it's on the fruitier side, but any chile flake or even black pepper will do.

3
Feel free to swap in other raw root vegetables here; celery root is a particular favorite.

Crunchy-Creamy Kohlrabi + Apple Salad

Shaving root veg on a mandoline is one of our favorite techniques for bringing a little lightness to the winter season's hardiest produce. In this cold-weather salad, kohlrabi and apple make a stellar slicey duo, at once sturdy and refreshing. The macadamia nuts are a fun left-of-center addition, a surprising bright light during the darkest (in solstice terms) days of the year. This is quite the juicy salad because we think this creamy celery seed vinaigrette is next-level delicious—we may even be guilty of enjoying it by the spoonful.

Celery Seed Vinaigrette

2 teaspoons mustard powder

¼ cup diced white onion (about ¼ onion)

½ teaspoon celery seeds

2 teaspoons kosher salt

2 teaspoons sugar

¼ cup distilled white vinegar

½ cup neutral oil, such as canola or sunflower

Salad

2 or 3 kohlrabi, peeled and thinly shaved
    on a mandoline

1 teaspoon kosher salt

1 or 2 crisp apples, such as Granny Smith or
    Honeycrisp, thinly shaved on a mandoline

¼ cup chopped macadamia nuts

1 **Make the celery seed vinaigrette:** In a blender, combine the mustard powder, onion, celery seeds, salt, sugar, and vinegar and blend on high speed until smooth, 15 to 20 seconds.

2 Reduce the speed to medium and slowly stream in the neutral oil. As soon as the oil has been incorporated, turn off the blender.[1] Set the vinaigrette aside.

3 **Assemble the salad:** In a medium bowl, sprinkle the shaved kohlrabi with the salt and toss with your hands (or a pair of tongs) to coat. Let it sit for a minute to soften the kohlrabi.

4 Holding the kohlrabi back with your hand, pour out any excess water that has accumulated at the bottom of the bowl. Add the shaved apples and the vinaigrette and toss. Add the macadamia nuts and toss again. Serve immediately.

1

Once you add the oil, you don't want to run the blender for any longer than you need to or you run the risk of breaking your emulsified (i.e., creamy) vinaigrette.

Broccoli with Pumpkin-Seed Jazz

The term "jazz" originated with cookbook author extraordinaire Molly Baz, which won't be surprising to anyone familiar with her singularly charming way with words. Molly worked with us at Glasserie back in 2013, and we're ever grateful for this addition to our culinary lexicon. Our "jazz" is usually made with ground nuts or seeds mixed with spices—not dissimilar from dukkah, the Middle Eastern condiment. We like to use jazz to dress up vegetables, and because it's always at least partially ground, it quickly comes together into a saucy coating. In this recipe, we toss the pumpkin-seed jazz with perfectly cooked broccoli. If you want to make broccoli toast—and we know you do— this makes a good amount for two very hefty or four more modest toasts. Fry slices of thick-cut, crusty bread in olive oil and slather them with labneh before piling the broccoli sky-high.

Get Ahead

If you omit the garlic from the jazz, it can be made a week or two in advance and stored in a sealed container at room temperature.

The jazzed broccoli holds well at room temperature or in the fridge for a couple hours, but it really is better the same day.

Pumpkin-Seed Jazz

½ cup pumpkin seeds
1½ teaspoons olive oil
½ garlic clove, grated on a Microplane
¼ teaspoon kosher salt
1 teaspoon Aleppo pepper

Broccoli

½ cup kosher salt
2 small or 1 large head broccoli,
    cut into large florets[1]
2 tablespoons olive oil
1 tablespoon lemon juice
    (about ½ lemon)
1 tablespoon orange juice

For Serving

¼ cup pomegranate seeds
¼ cup mint leaves

1 **Make the pumpkin-seed jazz:** Preheat the oven to 300°F.

2 In a small bowl, stir together the pumpkin seeds and olive oil. Spread onto a baking sheet and toast in the oven until deeply golden brown, 50 to 60 minutes, tossing halfway through. Remove from the oven and let cool to room temperature.

3 In a food processor (or using a mortar and pestle), combine the toasted pumpkin seeds, grated garlic, salt, and Aleppo. Pulse to a fine pebble (30 to 45 seconds' worth of pulsing), being careful not to grind into pumpkin-seed butter.

4 **Cook the broccoli:** In a large pot, bring 3 quarts water and the salt to a boil. Line a plate with paper towels. Add the broccoli and blanch[2] for 1 to 2 minutes, tasting for tenderness.[3] Using a spider or slotted spoon, remove the broccoli from the water, and place on the paper towels to drain, allowing it to fully dry.

5 In a cast-iron skillet, heat 1 tablespoon of the oil over medium-high heat. Add the broccoli and let it cook, untouched, for 5 minutes to get good color. Turn and cook the other side for 2 to 3 minutes more. Remove from the heat and let cool to room temperature.

6 In a large bowl, vigorously toss together the broccoli, the jazz, remaining 1 tablespoon olive oil, the lemon juice, and orange juice.

7 **To serve:** Before serving, top the broccoli with the pomegranate seeds and mint.

1
You can use the tender heart of the broccoli stems; they're arguably the best part. Just trim back the tough exterior around the stem, cut into bite-size pieces, and blanch along with the florets.

2
Blanching is the term for cooking something (most often a vegetable) in boiling water, often in advance of doing something else with it. Why not say "boiled"? Well, it's just not a very lovely term, is it?

3
Doneness is subjective here. You may like your broccoli more snappy or more tender than we do. Always taste to make sure it's where you want it, keeping in mind that it'll continue to cook from residual heat just a little more while it cools.

The Power of Raw Garlic

Garlic is one of the foundations of all cooking, full stop. It's welcome in so many places, from salad dressings to marinades, but it might just shine brightest when a whisper of it is added raw to finished food—there's nothing that quite compares.

The pleasant sharpness and earthy funk of raw garlic send a roasted vegetable or a pot of cooked beans into a category all its own. We often make garlic oil with just a little raw grated garlic whisked into olive oil and then brush it on anything from grilled romaine to sweet potatoes. Raw garlic's power is *the* way to make an aioli or a tahini sauce sing. It brings life and depth, paradoxically both lifting and grounding for the palate.

While maybe an obvious technique to point out, we've found that people just don't think about it much. We want you to rely on it as an indispensable technique from here on out.

As an experiment in seeing the difference, make the pumpkin-seed jazz for this broccoli salad (opposite) without adding the garlic at first. Taste it, consider it, then add the garlic, mix thoroughly, and let sit for a few minutes to mellow. Then taste it again. You'll really see the impact, and we hope you appreciate it as much as we do!

As with everything, quality is key. With garlic in this context, you want fresh, whole-head garlic only. Nothing prepeeled, or in a jar, or frozen for a fresh-garlic application. And ideally the heads are reasonably fresh, too. You don't want to see any green sprouting from the cloves. Old garlic is bitter and pungent and will turn this whole raw-garlic-is-life argument on its head.

Why We Love Flower Waters

If rose water and orange blossom water aren't already in your pantry, we'd love to encourage their inclusion. Flower waters are made through a process called steam distillation, which is the best way to extract the clear essence of the delicate flavors. We like to think of them as we would a spice, adding another layer of flavor to a dish, a different dimension. Floral flavors swoop in at the very end, after you think you're done tasting everything and lift the dish into the realm of the ethereal. You swallow, and then the aroma, as if by surprise, jumps back into your nose—a bite's delayed delight. Too much flower water, though, and their perfume overpowers. Achieve the right balance, and you're walking on air.

Radicchio Salad with Fennel-Roasted Fennel

Here it is, folks: the ideal winter salad! Doubling down, we roast fennel in a dusting of ground fennel seed, introduce it to some crunchy greens and tart apple, and finish with a flurry of nutty cheese over the top. It makes a satisfying lunch with a piece of toast or holds its own as a perfect partner to a roast chicken. Don't let the orange blossom water in the dressing send you running. The flavor here isn't overly floral, and it's balanced out by the nutty cheese and bitter greens. You'll wonder why you weren't splashing a little flower water into your salads before now.

Get Ahead

You can preroast the fennel a day or two ahead. Bring it out of the fridge for 40 minutes or so to come to room temperature before serving. You don't want it to be cold-cold.

Roasted Fennel

2 bulbs fennel, halved, ends trimmed, and cut into ¼-inch-thick slices
½ cup olive oil[1]
2 teaspoons kosher salt
2 tablespoons ground fennel seeds
¼ teaspoon fennel pollen (optional)

Dressing

Grated zest of 1 orange
2 tablespoons orange juice
Grated zest of ½ lemon, preferably a Meyer lemon
¼ cup lemon juice, preferably from Meyer lemons (about 2 lemons)
1 tablespoon whole-grain mustard
½ teaspoon orange blossom water
¼ cup olive oil
2 teaspoons kosher salt
½ teaspoon honey

Salad

1 tart apple, such as Pink Lady or Granny Smith, thinly sliced
1 to 3 heads radicchio (depending upon their size), leaves separated
Pecorino Romano cheese,[2] for grating

1 **Roast the fennel:** Place a baking sheet in the oven and preheat the oven to 450°F to get the pan ripping hot.[3]

2 In a medium bowl, toss the sliced fennel with the olive oil, salt, ground fennel seeds, and fennel pollen (if using) to coat evenly.

3 Remove the pan from the oven and carefully transfer the fennel mixture to the hot pan, spreading it out evenly. Roast until tender and browned on the edges, about 30 minutes. Remove from the oven and let cool to room temperature.

4 **Make the dressing:** In a small bowl, whisk together the orange zest, orange juice, lemon zest, lemon juice, mustard, orange blossom water, olive oil, salt, and honey.

5 **Assemble the salad:** In a large salad bowl, toss the apple and radicchio leaves with the dressing, then add in the roasted fennel and toss all together.

6 Arrange the dressed salad on a platter. Use a Microplane to grate a generous amount of the pecorino over the salad.

1
This seems like a lot of oil, we know. Once in the oven though, the fennel's going to want it all.

2
You won't need the whole hunk, just grab whatever you find from a store — they're usually sold in 4- to 8-ounce chunks. Ultimately, you decide how much cheese you want on your salad, but if you're anything like us, you'll want a heavy snowfall.

3
The idea here is to get really good caramelization on the fennel by heating up the tray first.

An Unlikely Shrimp Salad

Gently poached shrimp is one of the purest joys out there. Hyperbolic? We don't think so. The delicate spring of biting into a distillation of ocean-y umami—there's not a whole lot that beats it. Here, we've paired it with a perhaps curious partner: sliced apple. Stick with us; it's really very good. Tossed with a punchy fish sauce/lime dressing and fresh herbs, it may just convert you into something you never saw coming: a shrimp-and-apple-salad lover.

¼ cup plus 2 teaspoons kosher salt

1½ pounds medium shrimp, tails removed, halved horizontally[1]

¼ cup olive oil

3 tablespoons lime juice (1 or 2 limes)

2 teaspoons ground black lime[2]

2 teaspoons fish sauce

3 green apples, thinly shaved (on a mandoline, if possible)

1 cup dill leaves

1 cup mint leaves

1 In a medium saucepan, bring 6 cups water and ¼ cup of the salt to a boil. Turn off the heat, add the shrimp, and let poach for 60 to 90 seconds.[3]

2 Using a spider or slotted spoon, transfer the shrimp from the water to a plate, spreading in a single layer. Place in the fridge to cool for 30 minutes.

3 In a large bowl, combine the olive oil, lime juice, remaining 2 teaspoons salt, the ground black lime, and fish sauce and swirl or whisk together.

4 When the shrimp are cooled, lift them off the plate with a slotted spoon, being careful not to include any water that has accumulated, and transfer to a medium bowl. Add the shaved apple and dressing and toss gently, being careful not to break apart the apples.

5 Add the dill and mint, lightly toss, and serve.

1

Raw shrimp can be a little slippery and sticky to cut, so we recommend using a sharp knife, which you'll want to wipe down frequently to help move things along.

2

Black lime—aka dried lime—is a bit of a niche ingredient, and you can omit it, but you really shouldn't. You can find it at most spice shops and all Persian markets, or order it online from Burlap & Barrel.

3

Avoid rubbery shrimpies! You're looking for just-poached, tender shrimp.

Tomato-Lovers' Chicken Salad

This salad's got that summer feeling. Loaded with ripe and tasty tomatoes, hunks of juicy poached chicken, and a chile vinaigrette, it's perfect for those sweatier days of the year. We simply cannot sing the praises of this spicy vin enough: Fennel and coriander mingle with Aleppo pepper and tangy sumac, and the hit of raw garlic with sharp lemon juice keeps things exceptionally lively. No question this is a meal for tomato lovers, but it might actually be for the chile vinaigrette aficionados among us.

Get Ahead

The spiced oil for the vinaigrette can be made up to 3 days in advance and stored in the fridge. Just wait to add the lemon juice until ready to use.

1½ to 2 pounds boneless, skinless chicken breasts

2 bay leaves

2 garlic cloves, smashed

2 tablespoons olive oil

1 tablespoon kosher salt

Chile Vinaigrette

½ cup olive oil

1 clove garlic, grated on a Microplane

1 tablespoon Aleppo pepper

2 teaspoons sumac

1¼ teaspoons ground coriander

1¼ teaspoons ground fennel seeds

¾ teaspoon kosher salt

½ teaspoon freshly ground black pepper

¼ teaspoon ground cardamom

3 tablespoons lemon juice (about 1½ lemons)

Salad

¼ yellow onion, thinly sliced

3 small red tomatoes or 1 large heirloom, cut into wedges

1 bunch of arugula, stems trimmed

½ cup cilantro leaves[1]

½ cup parsley leaves[2]

1 In a medium saucepan, place the chicken breasts in a single layer. Add 2 cups cold water, the bay leaves, garlic cloves, olive oil, and salt. Cover the pot and bring the liquid up to a simmer over medium heat, about 10 minutes. Turn off the heat and, with the pot still covered, allow the chicken to gently cook for 20 minutes. Uncover and let the chicken cool in the liquid for 30 minutes.

2 Transfer the chicken to a plate. Discard the liquid (or reserve for another purpose, like soup). Using your hands, shred the chicken into large pieces and set aside.

3 **Make the chile vinaigrette:** In a small saucepan, heat the oil and garlic over low heat, swirling frequently, until lightly golden, 5 to 8 minutes. Turn off the heat.

4 Add the Aleppo, sumac, coriander, fennel, salt, black pepper, and cardamom and swirl the pan, letting the spices bloom in the hot oil for 30 seconds. Transfer to a large bowl and stir in the lemon juice.

5 **Assemble the salad:** Add the shredded chicken, sliced onion, and tomato wedges to the bowl with the vinaigrette and toss to coat. Add the arugula, cilantro, and parsley and lightly toss before serving.

1
Leaving a little stem on the cilantro is something you want to do. No need to be too careful.

2
If you want to change it up, any mix of soft herbs will get the job done. Mint, basil, tarragon, and cilantro are all great options. More esoteric herbs like lovage, summer savory, and chervil are fun alternatives as well.

As Good Tomorrow as It Is Today

We love having lots of small dishes to pick at: a variety of textures, colors, and flavors on the table. This snacky style of eating is us in a nutshell. The recipes in this chapter are all marinated little dishes that are delicious right away but really come into their own as they sit, harmonizing as they hang. You can eat them immediately or store them in the fridge for a future mix-and-match spread.

Chile Oil Pickles

When preservation legend Sandor Katz came out with a video series called *People's Republic of Fermentation*, I was hypnotized. A show that tied together both Chinese food *and* fermentation?! I couldn't watch it fast enough.

While watching the episode on doubanjiang, fermented broad bean–chile paste (one of my all-time favorite ingredients), I was inspired by the way the chiles were fermented and then sun-dried. Around this same time, I enjoyed a sandwich from an Armenian shop near Kismet that was filled with the fenugreek-spiced dried sausage called basturma. This chile oil is inspired by the flavors of both these preserved foods.

At Kismet, we ferment, dry, and then age Fresno peppers, but here we speed things up by using store-bought Calabrian chiles. These are added to spices toasted in olive oil to create a quick—and addictive—marinade for pickled vegetables. If you don't have time to pickle your own veg, buy some and skip straight to marinating! —Sarah Hymanson

Pickled Veggies[1]

2 carrots, halved lengthwise then
    into 2-inch spears
2 garlic cloves
¼ head cauliflower, cut into 2-inch florets
½ bulb fennel, cut into ¼-inch wedges
1½ cups distilled white vinegar
2 tablespoons kosher salt
2 tablespoons sugar
½ teaspoon ground turmeric
1 bay leaf

Chile Fenugreek Oil

¼ cup olive oil
1 garlic clove, grated on a Microplane
1 teaspoon ground fenugreek
1 teaspoon ground cumin
½ teaspoon freshly ground black pepper
2 tablespoons chopped Calabrian chiles

1   **Pickle the veggies:** In a tall, heatproof container or jar, place the carrots, garlic, cauliflower, and fennel.

2   In a small saucepan, combine 1½ cups water with the vinegar, salt, sugar, turmeric, and bay leaf and bring to a boil over medium heat. Pour this over the veggies and let sit uncovered at room temperature for 1 hour. Cover and refrigerate for at least 1 full day before using.

3   **Make the chile fenugreek oil:** In a small saucepan, combine the olive oil, grated garlic, fenugreek, cumin, and black pepper. Cook over low heat, swirling frequently, until the garlic browns lightly and the spices are fragrant, about 5 minutes.

4   Add the chiles and stir to combine. Remove from the heat and set aside.

5   To serve, drain the pickled vegetables in a colander and discard the liquid (or save in the fridge for a month or two for future pickling!). In a medium bowl, combine the drained pickles with the chile fenugreek oil. Let marinate at room temperature for at least 30 minutes or hold in the fridge[2] for up to 3 days.

1
You can use any mix of hearty vegetables; turnips and radishes are good choices, too.

2
If you're pulling the marinated pickles from the fridge, let them come to room temp for at least 30 minutes to take the chill off the oil before serving.

Mussels with Pickled Shallots

Bright, tangy, and a little sweet, these shallot-y mussels are an ideal appetizer alongside some good bread and butter. This dish came together in a flurry the day before Kismet's debut, in the fog of restaurant-opening exhaustion. Therefore, we remember nothing about how or why we created it. We were blessed by the mussel gods and never looked back.

Pickled Shallots

2 small shallots, sliced into thin rounds
1 tablespoon dried currants
¼ cup white wine vinegar
½ teaspoon coriander seeds
¼ teaspoon black peppercorns
1 tablespoon plus 1 teaspoon sugar
2 teaspoons kosher salt
½ teaspoon thyme leaves
Grated zest of ¼ orange
¼ cup olive oil

Mussels

1 tablespoon olive oil
2 sprigs thyme
2 pounds mussels
1 cup parsley leaves

1   **Make the pickled shallots:** In a small heatproof bowl, combine the shallots and currants.

2   In a small saucepan, combine the vinegar, 2 tablespoons water, the coriander, peppercorns, sugar, and salt and bring to a boil over medium heat. Pour the hot pickling liquid through a fine-mesh sieve over the shallots and currants. Discard the aromatics. Allow to pickle 5 to 10 minutes, then add the thyme leaves, orange zest, and the ¼ cup of olive oil to the pickled shallots and stir to combine.

3   **Prepare the mussels:** In a wide saucepan, combine ⅓ cup water, the 1 tablespoon olive oil, and thyme sprigs, and bring to a boil over high heat. Add the mussels in a single layer and cover the pan. Keep the lid on for the first 2 to 3 minutes, allowing the mussels to steam. As they begin to open, pull them out and place in a medium serving bowl. Cook until all of the mussels have opened.

4   Once all of the mussels have been removed from the pan, strain the cooking liquid through a fine-mesh sieve into a medium bowl. Place the bowl into the freezer to cool for 10 to 15 minutes, until the cooking liquid is no longer hot.

5   Pick each mussel from its shell, being careful to also remove the beard,[1] and place the mussels in a bowl. Discard the shells.

6   Pour ¼ cup of the cooled cooking liquid over the mussels, being careful to hold back any grit or residue from the bottom of the bowl. Stir the pickled shallot mixture into the mussels. Toss lightly with the parsley just before serving.[2]

1
The beard is the little fibrous ropy bit that mussels use to attach themselves to things. Not every mussel will have one, but look for it in the center on the open side after cooking. Be careful to hold the meat of the mussel as you remove the beard so you don't end up pulling the interior out with it. You'll get the hang of it after a few tries!

2
These shine the minute they're made but also keep well in the fridge for a day or two. Just hold off on adding the parsley until ready to serve.

Orangey Bay
+ Coriander Carrots

Brighton Beach is not popular among my sun-loving New York friends, but I love it for its exceptional Eastern European food and amazing people-watching, so sometimes my friends humor me.

One of my favorite places for beach snacks is the Brighton Bazaar. It's an endless trove of post–Soviet era treats, including but not limited to brown-bread croutons flavored with crab or bacon; frozen strawberry-cheesecake bars enrobed in chocolate; slices of salty salami; and a cornucopia of pickles, salads, and slaws, my favorite of which is known as "Korean salad."

It is a perfect carrot salad: crunchy, sweet, garlicky, and a little spicy. While its origin is fuzzy, it's at pretty much every Russian supermarket, a marker of the influence of Russia's once-substantial Korean population (that now largely resides in Central Asia). It's so good that friends don't mind making the trek. This recipe is an ode to that salad. —Sarah Hymanson

Get Ahead

The bay oil can be made up to 1 month ahead and kept covered in the fridge. It can be used in a multitude of ways: as part of a marinade, spooned over labneh, or tossed with your favorite root veg before roasting.

---

2 pounds carrots, scrubbed, ends trimmed

2 tablespoons kosher salt

¼ cup neutral oil, such as canola or sunflower

4 bay leaves

2 garlic cloves, grated on a Microplane

Grated zest of ½ orange

2 tablespoons orange juice

¼ cup white wine vinegar

1 tablespoon sugar

1 tablespoon plus 1 teaspoon Aleppo pepper

2 tablespoons coriander seeds, toasted and cracked[1]

¼ cup dill leaves

1. Fit a food processor with the grating blade and shred the carrots. (Alternatively, you can shred them on a mandoline with a julienne blade, cut them by hand, or shred on the large holes of a box grater.)

2. In a medium bowl, combine the shredded carrots and salt and toss well with your hands, massaging the salt into the carrots.[2] Toss every 10 minutes until a significant amount of liquid has pooled at the bottom of the bowl, about 30 minutes. Using your hands, squeeze any excess juice from the carrots and transfer them into a separate medium bowl.[3]

3. In a small saucepan, gently warm the oil and bay leaves over low heat for 10 minutes to infuse. Let cool to room temperature, then discard the bay leaves.

4. In a small bowl, whisk together the bay-infused oil, the grated garlic, orange zest, orange juice, vinegar, sugar, Aleppo, and coriander.

5. Pour the dressing over the carrots and toss well. Top with dill before serving.

---

[1] The texture of cracked coriander here is extra-pleasant. Toast coriander seeds in a small sauté pan over medium-low heat, swirling occasionally, until fragrant, 3 to 5 minutes. Let cool, then crack by pulsing in a spice grinder or in a mortar and pestle. If all you have is ground coriander, that's just fine, too.

[2] By salting the carrots first, you're drawing out the liquid. This technique ensures your salad won't become a watery mess.

[3] You can use the salty carrot liquid to marinate chicken, dress other vegetables, cook rice, or add to a veg stock. Or toss it!

Spiced Winter Squash with Walnuts

Do you steam your veg? If not, you're going to want to get in the habit. Steaming is perhaps the most elegant way of preparing vegetables. We particularly love a steam for kabocha squash: It's fast, precise, and delicate, yielding incomparably supple squash. Just after steaming, the hot squash is tossed with our version of hawaij, an earthy spice blend of Yemeni origin. Wilt in the arugula at the end for a veg dish that's heaven right away and holds for days.

1 cup walnuts

½ kabocha squash, cut into ¾-inch wedges (about 4 cups)

1½ teaspoons kosher salt

1 teaspoon ground turmeric

¾ teaspoon ground cumin

½ teaspoon ground coriander

½ teaspoon freshly ground black pepper

¼ teaspoon ground cardamom

¼ teaspoon ground caraway

¼ cup olive oil

3 tablespoons apple cider vinegar

2 tablespoons pomegranate molasses

4 cups arugula, stems trimmed

1 Preheat the oven to 275°F.

2 Spread the walnuts on a baking sheet and toast for 30 to 40 minutes.[1] Set aside to cool, then roughly chop.

3 In a medium bowl, toss the squash pieces with 1 teaspoon of the salt. Let sit for 10 minutes for the salt to fully dissolve.

4 Fill a large pot with 2 inches of water and set a colander inside (or set up a steamer). Cover and bring water to a boil, then reduce the heat to a simmer. Add the squash in a single layer, cover, and steam until tender, 10 to 12 minutes. Transfer to a serving dish.[2]

5 In a small bowl, combine the turmeric, cumin, coriander, black pepper, cardamom, caraway, and remaining ½ teaspoon salt. Whisk in the oil, vinegar, and pomegranate molasses.

6 Pour the dressing over the squash and gently mix to coat evenly. Add the arugula and lightly toss to wilt it. Top with the toasted walnuts.

1
For a little extra oomph, lightly coat the walnuts in a splash of olive oil and sprinkle with salt before toasting.

2
Depending upon the size of your pot or steamer, you may need to do this in batches.

Presalt
Your Vegetables

Why do we season the summer squash in this recipe 20 minutes before sautéing it? It helps to understand a little basic science!

Through a process called osmosis, water will always move from areas with less salt to areas with more. Tossing vegetables with salt therefore pulls the liquid out of them. This serves us in a few ways:

• Vegetables with less water have a more concentrated flavor.

• When making a salad, salting any juicy vegetables first helps avoid diluting the vinaigrette.

• Water hinders the process of caramelization, so if you're looking for crispy, browned veg, the faster you get rid of the water, the better.

• Evenly salting a particularly craggy vegetable, like cauliflower, can be hard. By letting the salt sit for 20 minutes, you give it a chance to draw out enough water to create a little brine, which can then seep into all of the nooks.

Presalting comes up again and again in our kitchens, and we hope you look to it as a very helpful hack for many different veg applications once you develop a feel for it.

Summer Squash in Buttermilk Dressing

This salad is loosely Turkish-inspired, and if you really want to feel like you're in Istanbul, we recommend it next to a glass of raki, the national drink of Turkey. (If not raki, any anise-y spirit you can get your hands on is just dandy.) There's also a strong argument to be made that this salad is best at breakfast, with toast and a soft-boiled egg, booze optional.

2 or 3 summer squash,[1] cut or shaved on a mandoline into ⅛-inch-thick rounds (about 6 cups)
2 teaspoons kosher salt
1 tablespoon olive oil

Dressing
⅓ cup goat cheese, at room temperature
½ cup buttermilk
1 teaspoon kosher salt
1 teaspoon olive oil
Grated zest of ¼ lemon
1 tablespoon lemon juice (about ½ lemon)
½ teaspoon dried oregano or ¼ teaspoon fresh
½ garlic clove, grated on a Microplane

1 In a medium bowl, combine the sliced squash and salt and toss to evenly distribute. Let sit for 20 minutes, then squeeze the water from the squash using your hands.

2 In a medium skillet, heat the olive oil over high heat. Add the squash and quickly sauté to soften, 3 to 5 minutes, stirring often, and taking care not to let it brown. Transfer to a medium bowl and set aside to cool to room temperature.

3 **Make the dressing:** In a medium bowl, whisk together the goat cheese, buttermilk, salt, olive oil, lemon zest, lemon juice, oregano, and garlic.

4 Toss the dressing with the squash and serve.

1
We used zucchini in the photo (fun fact: zucchini are summer squash!), but we love summer squash in all shapes and sizes, and we support using any variety in this recipe: Gold Bar squash, avocado squash, pattypan squash. . . .

Hibiscus + Beets: A Love Story

Over the years, we've often used hibiscus as a tangy best friend for beets. Iliana Loza, Kismet sous-chef extraordinaire, helped workshop this shining example of how well the two ingredients play together, tossing roasted beets with sweet-salty hibiscus flowers. We swirl in crème fraîche for a lightly creamy ode to a cool bowl of borscht.

3 medium beets (each about the size of a tennis ball)

2½ teaspoons kosher salt

1 tablespoon olive oil, plus more for finishing

1 bay leaf

1 cup dried hibiscus flowers

1 tablespoon sugar

⅓ cup crème fraîche

Pinch of ground nutmeg (about 6 swipes on a Microplane grater, if using whole nutmeg)

1　Preheat the oven to 425°F.

2　Place a large piece of foil loosely in a small ovenproof dish. Add the beets with 1 teaspoon of the salt, the olive oil, and bay leaf. Using your hands, rub the oil and salt into the beets to coat, top with 2 tablespoons water, and wrap up in the foil.

3　Transfer the dish to the oven and roast until tender, 1 hour to 1 hour 15 minutes. Unwrap the beets and pierce them with a knife to check that they're tender all the way through. Remove the dish from the oven and open the foil to allow the steam to escape.

4　Once cool enough to handle, peel the beets and cut them into bite-size pieces.

5　In a small bowl, combine the dried hibiscus with 1 cup water, agitating the hibiscus well before removing it to let any attached grit fall to the bottom. Remove the hibiscus from the water and rinse thoroughly.

6　In a medium saucepan, combine the hibiscus, sugar, remaining 1½ teaspoons salt, and 1 cup fresh water and bring to a boil over medium-high heat. Reduce to a simmer, stirring intermittently, until the hibiscus is tender (but still chewy), 10 to 15 minutes.

7　In a medium serving bowl, combine the beets and hibiscus (along with its liquid). Add the crème fraîche and nutmeg and swirl together.

8　Serve immediately or chill in the fridge for up to 5 days. Either way, top with a dash of olive oil before serving.

Sweet + Spicy Eggplant

This recipe is tangy, sweet, and spicy—truly everything you want in a marinated eggplant. The key is steaming (rather than roasting or frying), which keeps the eggplant ethereally light. We developed this to be highly comforting and to travel with ease; it goes great with a picnic blanket, some Classic Tahini Sauce (page 116), and crusty bread.

2 Chinese eggplants, halved lengthwise,
    then each half cut crosswise into
    4 equal pieces

2½ teaspoons kosher salt

2 garlic cloves, finely chopped

2 tablespoons olive oil

2 teaspoons Aleppo pepper

¼ teaspoon freshly ground black pepper

1 teaspoon ground cumin

1 tablespoon pomegranate molasses[1]

1 tablespoon light brown sugar

1 tablespoon red wine vinegar

⅓ cup basil leaves

1   In a medium bowl, sprinkle the eggplant pieces with 1 teaspoon of the salt.

2   Fill a large pot with 2 inches of water and set a colander inside (or set up a steamer). Cover and bring the water to a boil. Working in batches, if necessary, place the eggplant in the steamer in a single layer and cook, covered, until knife-tender, about 10 minutes. Transfer to a plate to cool.

3   In a small saucepan, combine the garlic and olive oil and cook over medium-low heat, swirling the pan frequently to toast the garlic to golden brown, 3 to 4 minutes. Add the Aleppo, black pepper, and cumin and stir for 3 more minutes.

4   Remove the saucepan from the heat and let the mixture cool slightly. Add the remaining 1½ teaspoons salt, the pomegranate molasses, brown sugar, and vinegar and stir to dissolve.

5   Transfer the steamed eggplant to a medium serving bowl. Add the sauce and toss to combine. Sprinkle the basil leaves over the top, toss lightly, and serve.

[1]
You can substitute honey for
the pomegranate molasses;
add an extra splash of red
wine vinegar for tang.

Baharat-Roasted Mushrooms

The term *baharat* applies to a wide swath of spice blends across the Middle East and North Africa. This allspice-heavy baharat recipe makes more than you'll need, and we even suggest doubling or tripling it to have it on hand for anything from marinating meat to spicing up lentils. We especially love it with mushrooms. These tasty little maitake morsels make the perfect addition to any cheese plate. They also make a swell sidekick to a bit of steak or chicken for a quick dinner.

Roasted Mushrooms

14 to 16 ounces fresh maitake mushrooms, broken into chunks[1]

1 yellow onion, cut into 6 wedges

¾ cup olive oil

2 teaspoons baharat (recipe follows)

3 bay leaves

4 sprigs thyme

1 tablespoon kosher salt

2 teaspoons red wine vinegar

¼ cup dried cherries

Baharat

2 teaspoons ground allspice

1 teaspoon ground coriander

¼ teaspoon ground cumin

¼ teaspoon ground cardamom

¼ teaspoon ground cinnamon

¼ teaspoon ground cloves

¼ teaspoon freshly ground black pepper

1   Preheat the oven to 375°F.

2   **Roast the mushrooms:** On a baking sheet, toss the mushrooms and onion with the olive oil, baharat, bay leaves, thyme, and salt and spread out in an even layer. Bake until browned, 50 to 60 minutes, tossing halfway through.

3   Remove from the oven and add the vinegar and cherries to the pan, tossing gently with tongs.

4   Serve warm or at room temperature.

Baharat

In a small bowl, whisk together the allspice, coriander, cumin, cardamom, cinnamon, cloves, and black pepper.

1
You're looking for nice chunks of maitakes, not a bunch of frilly flakes. Break them apart using your hands, or gently use a knife to cut apart the base evenly and then pull them apart from bottom to top.

Our Take on Marinated Artichokes

Marinated artichoke hearts are arguably the most decadent treat of the vegetable world, the star of aperitivo hours and mezze spreads everywhere. The hearts are a well-protected prize nestled inside a fortress of leathery leaves. Battling your way to the core is a labor of love, but it's a worthy undertaking. Artichoke hearts are so delicious that they don't need much to shine, but ours get the special treatment: a heavy dose of toasted garlic, fragrant orange zest, and a dash of fish sauce.

If you've never trimmed an artichoke down to the heart, you might want to consult the internet. It's tedious, yes, but fun once you get the hang of it—one of those gloriously meditative kitchen activities. We recommend making it a group activity or putting on a colorful podcast for company.

1 lemon, halved
4 large or 8 small artichokes

Marinade
2 garlic cloves, grated on a Microplane
¼ cup olive oil
¼ teaspoon freshly ground black pepper
⅛ teaspoon nigella seeds
½ teaspoon fish sauce
Pinch of grated orange zest
2 teaspoons lemon juice

Artichoke Hearts
⅓ cup lemon juice (2 to 2½ lemons)
¼ cup olive oil
3 tablespoons kosher salt
5 garlic cloves, smashed
2 bay leaves
2 sprigs tarragon
2 tablespoons honey

1 Set up a large bowl filled with water and squeeze the lemon into the water. Lop off the bottom of the stem and then the top half of each artichoke. Trim it down to the heart by snapping off and then paring back the thick outer leaves until you've reached the tender core. Trim the outer stem down to the tender center, then cut the heart in half, lengthwise. Carve out the inedible, prickly center, then place each prepped artichoke into the lemon water as you continue to work.

2 **Make the marinade:** In a small saucepan, combine the grated garlic and olive oil and cook over medium-low heat, swirling frequently until the garlic is lightly browned, 6 to 8 minutes.

3 Remove from the heat and add the black pepper and nigella seeds. Transfer to a medium bowl. Add the fish sauce, orange zest, and lemon juice and whisk to combine. Set aside.

4 **Cook the artichoke hearts:** In a large pot, combine 6 cups water, the lemon juice, olive oil, salt, smashed garlic, bay leaves, tarragon, and honey. Bring to a boil, then reduce to a simmer. Add the cleaned artichoke hearts and lightly simmer for 15 to 20 minutes, until tender.[1]

5 Using a slotted spoon, remove the artichoke hearts from the pot and place into the prepared marinade, along with ¼ cup of the cooking liquid.

6 Serve at room temperature (this will hold for up to 4 hours) or transfer to the fridge until ready to serve.[2]

[1] Stab a piece of artichoke with a sharp paring knife to determine when it's tender. Your knife should pierce it easily without sticking.

[2] If you're saving the marinated artichokes for another day, be sure to pull them from the fridge an hour before serving. They're definitely best at room temp.

Squid Salad, but Make It Couscous

Pearl couscous is an often overlooked grain (well, technically pasta). It's all springy bounce, serving up chewy comfort in every bite. We make a tomatoey couscous salad at Rotisserie that's very similar to this one, and it's been a hit from day one. Adding squid makes this version a little more deluxe—a great dish to show off to company but casual enough for a picnic in the park.

Couscous

¼ cup olive oil

3 garlic cloves, sliced

1 cup pearl couscous

1 tablespoon tomato paste

1 teaspoon kosher salt

1 teaspoon sumac

1 teaspoon Aleppo pepper

1 teaspoon paprika

½ teaspoon dried mint

½ teaspoon ground cumin

1 tablespoon sherry vinegar

Marinated Tomatoes

½ cup diced red onion (about ½ onion)

1 teaspoon kosher salt

1 tablespoon sherry vinegar

1 cup cherry tomatoes, halved

1 tablespoon olive oil

Squid

½ pound squid, tentacles[1] and tubes separated, tubes sliced into ¼- to ½-inch rings

½ teaspoon kosher salt

1 teaspoon olive oil

½ cup parsley leaves

1 **Cook the couscous:** In a medium saucepan, combine the olive oil and sliced garlic and cook over medium heat, swirling occasionally, until the garlic is lightly browned, about 4 minutes.

2 Add the couscous, tomato paste, salt, sumac, Aleppo, paprika, dried mint, and cumin. Stir well, then mix in the sherry vinegar and 1⅓ cups water.

3 Cover the pot and bring to a boil. Reduce to a simmer and cook for 10 minutes. Turn off the heat and let sit for 5 minutes, covered.

4 Spread the cooked couscous out onto a plate and cool to room temperature, about 25 minutes.

5 **Marinate the tomatoes:** In a large bowl, combine the diced onion, salt, and vinegar. Let sit for at least 5 minutes. Add the tomatoes and olive oil, toss together, and set aside.

6 **Prepare the squid:** Rinse the squid under cold water and dry them off on paper towels. In a small bowl, combine the squid with the salt and olive oil and mix to coat evenly.

7 Heat a large skillet over high heat for 2 minutes. Add the squid to the hot pan and cook for 1 to 2 minutes, shaking the pan back and forth to ensure even doneness. Using a slotted. spoon or tongs, add the cooked squid to the bowl with the tomatoes.

8 Mix in the couscous, stirring to combine. Fold in the parsley and serve.[2]

1
If the squid are particularly large, cut the tentacles into manageable pieces as well.

2
Highly recommend eating this salad at room temp. Cold pasta has its place, but we think this isn't it.

Dips + Sauces

We're very saucy people. Dry food? No thanks. We want sauce on everything. Even sauce is better with another sauce. Green zhoug with labneh? Yes. Garlic sauce with chile crisp? Game over. These are the schmears we couldn't live without.

Red Zhoug

It isn't a stretch to say that this fiery, garlic-lover's **Middle Eastern spice paste** is where it all began for me. This singular version of red zhoug is *the* culinary touchstone for my family, a condiment worth its weight in gold. As a kid, I'd eat this most weekends with malawach (page 224) and labneh (page 98), blissfully unaware of how intense this amount of raw garlic might come across to others; it was just what food was to me.

My mother learned this version of red zhoug from Hana Amiga (my father's best friend's mother), who was an incredibly talented Yemeni-Israeli cook. She was a holy figure in her family—the ultimate matriarch. Sarah and I had the incredible privilege of cooking with her during a trip to Tel Aviv in 2014, before she passed away. The ease that she emanated in the kitchen was awe-inspiring, a graceful reflection of a life lived by the spoon.

To achieve the desired rustic, spice-studded, paste-like consistency, we use whole spices in this recipe, but if all you have are ground spices, don't let that stop you. Regardless, you'll end up with a spicy garlic bomb that you'll come to crave on everything from fried eggs to grilled chicken.
—Sara Kramer

1 tablespoon whole cardamom pods
2 tablespoons black peppercorns
2 tablespoons cumin seeds
4 arbol chiles, stems removed
2 tablespoons kosher salt
2 cups garlic cloves (from about 6 heads)
2 tablespoons olive oil, plus more
    for covering
1 medium tomato, peeled and seeded[1]

1 In a skillet, toast the cardamom, black peppercorns, cumin, and chiles over medium-low heat, swirling often to toast evenly, until fragrant, about 2 minutes.

2 Combine the toasted spices, chiles, and salt in a food processor[2] and run for about 90 seconds, until broken down. You should no longer see any whole spices, but they shouldn't be as fine as ground spices.

3 Add the garlic to the food processor and run for 1 to 2 minutes to break down the garlic into a paste with the spices, scraping down the sides as needed.

4 Add the olive oil and pulse for 10 to 15 seconds, scraping down the sides again. Add the tomato and run for another minute, scraping down as needed, to combine everything.

5 Store in the fridge, covered with a thin layer of olive oil, for up to 3 months.

1
If you want an efficient method for peeling a tomato, score the skin and quickly dip it into boiling water – afterwards, the peel slips right off. If not, just do your best to trim the skin off with a sharp knife. Or leave it on! It's getting blended, so peeling isn't crucial – it's just a nice touch.

2
You can also make this with a mortar and pestle (and a little elbow grease) if you happen to have that, in place of a food processor.

Green Zhoug

We always struggle with the best verbiage to describe zhoug. Is it a paste? Is it a sauce? Maybe it's a spicy salsa verde. Nothing quite captures it, but if we all make zhoug, then we'll all know what zhoug is like, right?

Zhoug is a classic falafel condiment, but if you make a batch to keep on hand for the week, you'll find yourself tossing it with roasted potatoes, mixing it in with tuna salad, or spooning it over a piece of fish. There is no shortage of zhoug (or schoug or zhug or schug) recipes out there, but this ultrafresh version is the one for us.

Get Ahead

This zhoug holds well for several days, particularly if you wait to add the lemon juice until just before serving. Bring the zhoug out of the fridge at least 30 minutes prior to serving it, as you'll want to make sure the oil isn't solid.

1½ cups (about 1 bunch) chopped cilantro, stems included[1]

½ cup (about ⅓ bunch) chopped parsley, stems included

2 serrano chiles, stemmed and seeded, chopped

2 garlic cloves, grated on a Microplane

1 teaspoon ground coriander

½ teaspoon ground cumin

¼ teaspoon ground cardamom

¼ teaspoon ground cloves

1½ teaspoons kosher salt

2 tablespoons lemon juice (about 1 lemon)

⅔ cup olive oil

1   In a food processor, combine the cilantro, parsley, serranos, garlic, coriander, cumin, cardamom, cloves, salt, lemon juice, and olive oil.

2   Run the food processor for 15 to 30 seconds, scraping down the sides as needed, until the mixture comes together into a chunky herb paste.

3   Store in the fridge until ready to serve.

[1]
As we're going full stem here, it's important to prechop the cilantro and parsley before adding them to the food processor, otherwise you're in for a world of stringy pain. These two are classic, but you can improvise with other herbs, like basil and dill.

For the Love of Labneh

This kefir-cultured labneh is our pride and joy at Kismet. There are lots of recipes for labneh out there, and most of them are, in fact, just strained yogurt. Here, we're culturing the dairy with kefir grains, and it's a whole different thing. Like all fermentation, this is a fun project worthy of a little patience. While delicious alone, labneh is also a perfect canvas for other flavors: We combine it with fresh horseradish, bay leaves, preserved lemon, or a "ranchy" mix of onion powder and dried mint. While we love the idea of getting you all aboard the fermentation train, all of these variations would be just as tasty using store-bought labneh in place of homemade.

Kismet Labneh

Kefir grains are the mysterious little fun-with-fermentation blobs that we use to culture fresh milk and cream into labneh. After several days, the dairy transforms, thickening and souring, at which point we remove the grains and drain off the liquid, resulting in the thick, spreadable kefir cheese known as labneh (or lebneh, lebni, or labaneh). The grains are endlessly reusable, and they continue to grow as you feed them (making them good gifts for fermentation-curious friends). Like any living thing, the grains need nourishment, so to keep them alive between batches, store them in milk in your fridge.

Get Ahead

As this is a fermented product, this labneh holds in the fridge for a long time, up to 1 month. It will continue to ferment, so if you're keeping it for longer than a few days (which is totally fine to do), you'll just want to give it a stir every so often.

4 cups heavy cream
2⅔ cups whole milk
1 tablespoon milk kefir grains[1]
1 teaspoon kosher salt

1   In a plastic or glass container with a lid, stir together the cream and milk.

2   Put the kefir grains into a cheesecloth sachet or a metal tea ball and add to the dairy mixture. Cover and let sit at room temperature for 2 to 4 days.[2] Stir and taste daily. During this time, the dairy will begin to thicken and sour.[3]

3   When you've achieved the desired level of sourness, around day 3 or 4, remove the sachet of grains, mix well, cover, and transfer the container to the fridge, to set up overnight.

4   Set a mesh sieve over a bowl and line it with a double layer of cheesecloth. Using a rubber spatula, and without mixing it, empty the dairy mixture into the cheesecloth. Tie up the ends of the cheesecloth over the labneh. Place the bowl with the sieve in the fridge overnight (or up to 2 nights for a very thick labneh). Then transfer the labneh to a bowl and season with salt.

[1]
There are two types of kefir grains: water and milk. You'll want to be sure you're getting the dairy version. They're easy to source online, or if you're lucky enough to have a fermentation shop nearby, they'll certainly have them.

[2]
The speed of fermentation largely depends upon the ambient temperature. The hotter it is, the faster it'll go.

[3]
The liquidy whey will start to separate from the thickening labneh. Nothing to worry about there. Give it a stir every day to keep things moving along nicely.

Horseradish Labneh

Fresh horseradish is the key to this slightly spicy, rich-n-creamy, good-on-anything sauce. We love it with a duck breast, atop a roasted sweet potato, or to up your roast beef sandwich game. In a pinch, using prepared horseradish works, but fresh is just a whole different world.

⅓ cup finely grated fresh horseradish
    (about 2 inches horseradish root
    grated on a Microplane)
2 tablespoons distilled white vinegar[1]
1½ teaspoons kosher salt
2 tablespoons olive oil
1 teaspoon fish sauce
¼ teaspoon freshly ground black pepper
2 cups labneh, store-bought or
    homemade (page 98)

1   In a medium bowl, combine the grated horseradish, vinegar, salt, olive oil, fish sauce, and black pepper and mix thoroughly.

2   Add the labneh to the bowl and mix together until homogeneous. Horseradish labneh will keep in the refrigerator, covered, for up to 1 week.

[1]
If using prepared horseradish,
omit the vinegar.

Bay Leaf Labneh

Anyone who questions the singular power of bay leaves will be swayed to the right side of history by this labneh. It's hard to describe just what makes bay leaves so special, but it's some combination of earthy spice and eucalyptus-y herbiness. Bay is a natural friend to dairy; combine it with rich and tangy labneh and you have the ideal accompaniment to crudités, fried eggs, or virtually any sandwich.

10 fresh bay leaves,[1] leaves stripped
    and ribs discarded
½ cup chopped parsley
½ cup olive oil
½ garlic clove, grated on a Microplane
2 cups labneh, store-bought or
    homemade (page 98)
1½ teaspoons kosher salt

1   In a blender, combine the bay leaves, parsley, olive oil, and grated garlic. Blend on high until smooth, 1 to 2 minutes, turning off the blender to scrape down the sides as needed.

2   Place a fine-mesh sieve over a medium bowl. Add the herb oil, using a rubber spatula to press on the solids to extract as much flavored oil as possible. Discard the solids.

3   Add the labneh and salt to the bowl with the oil, and use the rubber spatula to mix thoroughly to combine.

[1]
Unlike other recipes where we might permit a dried bay leaf, this recipe absolutely requires fresh.

Ranchy Labneh

You love labneh (or you wouldn't be reading this book), and like the rest of us, you want to dip most anything in ranch dressing. It makes sense that we'd arrive here: a marriage of two perfect foods. Ranchy labneh is the upgrade your celery sticks and wings deserve.

½ teaspoon onion powder

1½ teaspoons kosher salt

1 teaspoon dried mint

2 garlic cloves, grated on a Microplane

Grated zest of ¼ lemon

1 tablespoon lemon juice (about ½ lemon)

1 tablespoon olive oil

½ teaspoon Worcestershire sauce

2 cups labneh, store-bought or homemade (page 98)

In a medium bowl, combine the onion powder, salt, mint, garlic, lemon zest, lemon juice, olive oil, and Worcestershire. Add the labneh and mix together until homogeneous.

Preserved Lemon Labneh

Blending preserved lemon into a puree gives this labneh a particularly satiny feel. It's a dream as a dip for raw snap peas, or do what we do: Plate a heaping spoonful with a glug of honey and a generous pinch of Urfa pepper, and enjoy it next to a piece of malawach (page 224).

MAKES 2 CUPS

1 preserved lemon
2 cups labneh, store-bought or homemade (page 98)

1   Rinse the preserved lemon under cold water to remove the excess salt. Cut in half and remove the seeds.

2   In a blender, combine the preserved lemon and ½ cup water and blend on high until smooth.

3   In a medium bowl, combine the labneh and preserved lemon puree and mix until smooth.

Chile Crisp

The chile oil at Kismet Rotisserie has to be the most asked-about menu item among all our restaurants. A curious friend or customer asks us what's in it, no exaggeration, at least once a day. The spice blend is a little bit of sorcery, but the real secret is cinnamon.

This is the Rotisserie chile oil recipe, but with a higher crisp-to-oil ratio, hence the "chile crisp" designation. At home, we go full crisp.

1½ cups neutral oil, such as canola
    or sunflower
2 tablespoons chopped garlic
    (about 4 cloves)
⅓ cup gochugaru[1]
1 tablespoon crushed red pepper flakes
3 tablespoons Aleppo pepper
1 teaspoon ground turmeric
1 tablespoon ground coriander
1 teaspoon ground cinnamon
1 teaspoon ground cumin
1 teaspoon paprika
1 teaspoon freshly ground black pepper
1 teaspoon kosher salt

1   In a heavy-bottomed medium saucepan, combine the oil and garlic and cook over medium heat for 5 to 6 minutes, stirring constantly to ensure the garlic doesn't stick to the pot.

2   When the garlic just starts to get some golden color, remove from the heat and continue stirring for another 30 seconds.

3   Add the gochugaru, pepper flakes, Aleppo, turmeric, coriander, cinnamon, cumin, paprika, black pepper, and salt and stir to combine. Let cool to room temperature and store indefinitely in the fridge.

[1]
You can find gochugaru (Korean chile flakes) in Korean supermarkets and many grocery stores. If you have an abundance of Aleppo, or some other relatively mild chile flake, you can definitely use that instead. Italian-vibe crushed red pepper flakes are going to be a very spicy sub, but if you can handle the heat, they're an option, too.

Garlic Sauce

This garlic sauce, our version of a classic toum, lives at the heart of Kismet Rotisserie's popularity. To know Kismet Rotisserie is to love this garlic sauce. It gets served alongside every single chicken, and its talents don't stop there. Garlic sauce loves veggies, fish, and meat alike. Dip a pita in it! Garlic sauce does it all.

We adapted this recipe from a traditional Lebanese toum, blanching some of the garlic to soften its bite and using some sneaky instant mashed potatoes to help stabilize the sauce's emulsification. Speaking of keeping things stable, it helps to start out with cold ingredients.

½ cup plus 7 garlic cloves
1 tablespoon kosher salt
3 tablespoons lemon juice (about 1½ lemons)
¼ cup instant mashed potatoes[1]
1 cup neutral oil, such as sunflower or canola

1   Set up a small bowl filled with ice water. In a small saucepan, bring 2 cups water to a boil. Drop the ½ cup of garlic into the boiling water and cook for 3 minutes. Using a spider or slotted spoon, transfer the garlic to the ice bath for 1 minute, then remove.

2   In a blender, combine the cooked garlic, 7 cloves raw garlic, salt, lemon juice, and 3 tablespoons cold water. Blend on high until smooth, about 20 seconds. Add the instant mashed potatoes and blend for another 10 seconds.

3   With the blender still running on high, slowly stream in the oil to emulsify. Turn off the blender as soon as all of the oil is fully incorporated. Store, covered, for up to 1 week in the fridge.

[1]
Make sure to get the right ingredient here. We used Whole Foods brand instant mashed potatoes, but the Idahoan brand works just as well. Avoid anything that's powdered potato or potato starch.

Almond "Aioli"

Not a true aioli due to its lack of egg, but much like one, this faux-ioli is an everysauce—there's very little it won't pair well with. Moroccan-Spiced Carrots (page 142)? Indeed. The Only Way to Bake a Salmon (page 172)? That's the ticket.

MAKES 1½ CUPS

1 cup blanched or slivered almonds
1½ teaspoons kosher salt
1 garlic clove, grated on a Microplane
2 tablespoons lemon juice (about 1 lemon)
¼ cup olive oil

1   In a food processor,[1] combine the almonds and salt. Run until thoroughly broken down, about 1 minute, pausing to scrape down the sides.

2   Add the garlic, lemon juice, and ½ cup water and run until smooth and creamy looking, 1 to 2 minutes.

3   Transfer to a blender and blend on high until smooth. With the blender running, stream in the olive oil until just combined. It should be homogeneous and smooth with no streaks of oil.

1
If you have a high-powered blender, like a Vitamix, you can skip the food processor step. Use the blender's plunger to help move the almonds along.

Pine Nut Pepper Schmear

If ever there was a sauce to pair with a grilled chicken skewer, this is it. The combination of pine nuts and peppers evokes a smoky campfire on a summer night. Apart from grilled chicken, this schmear's pairing possibilities are endless: Try it with roasted cauliflower, sautéed green beans, grilled fish, or wherever your imagination takes you.

Get Ahead
Holds for up to 3 days in the fridge. It's great cold, or you can heat it up.

1 cup pine nuts
1 green bell pepper
1 jalapeño
1 garlic clove, grated on a Microplane
2 tablespoons plus 1 teaspoon lemon juice
    (about 1 lemon)
1½ teaspoons kosher salt
¼ cup olive oil

1   Preheat the oven to 275°F. Line a baking sheet with parchment paper.

2   Spread the pine nuts on the baking sheet and bake until lightly golden, 15 to 20 minutes.

3   Directly over an open flame (on your stove or grill), char the bell pepper and jalapeño, turning frequently with tongs, until blackened on all sides,[1] about 10 minutes.

4   Transfer the peppers to a bowl, cover with a plate, and let cool to room temperature, about 30 minutes.

5   Peel the skin from the peppers,[2] then cut them in half and remove and discard the stem, seeds, and excess liquid.

6   Transfer the peppers to a food processor and add the toasted pine nuts, grated garlic, lemon juice, and salt and process until smooth, scraping down the sides as needed. With the machine running, stream in the olive oil until fully incorporated and smooth.[3]

[1]
If the skins are not pretty thoroughly charred, they're much harder to peel.

[2]
If you're not using gloves, be careful about touching your eyes (and other parts) after handling spicy peppers.

[3]
If your pepper was on the smaller side, you might end up with a gluey schmear. You can thin it a bit with a tablespoon or two of water and/or a little extra lemon juice. Use your taste buds to guide you.

Peanut Muhammara

This is the muhammara recipe we developed for Kismet Rotisserie, subbing peanuts for the traditional walnuts for an Americana twist on this Middle Eastern dip of Syrian origin. It makes a primo sweet-spicy copilot to feta alongside some toasty bread or paired with grilled spring onions as an ode to the Catalan classic, calçots and romesco.

1½ cups peanuts

2 cups drained jarred piquillo peppers

2 yellow onions, diced

8 garlic cloves, smashed

1 tablespoon plus 1 teaspoon kosher salt

⅓ cup olive oil

1 tablespoon Aleppo pepper

2 teaspoons ground coriander

2 teaspoons ground cumin

2 teaspoons paprika

3 tablespoons sherry vinegar

2 tablespoons pomegranate molasses

1 Preheat the oven to 275°F.

2 Spread the peanuts on a baking sheet and toast for 30 minutes. Set aside to cool.

3 Leave the oven on and increase the temperature to 450°F.

4 In a baking dish,[1] combine the piquillos, onions, and garlic. Stir in the salt, olive oil, Aleppo, coriander, cumin, and paprika to evenly distribute. Roast in the oven for 40 minutes, stirring halfway through. (The veg should pick up a little char.) Remove from the oven and let cool to room temperature.

5 In a food processor, combine the roasted veg, peanuts, vinegar, and pomegranate molasses and run for a minute or two, scraping down the sides as needed, until smooth.[2]

---

[1] The veg should fit in the dish snugly. If your dish is bigger and they're more spread out, reduce the cooking time.

[2] The consistency should be pretty smooth but not a silky puree. If chunky is your preference, a little texture never hurt anyone.

Tahini Is Life

Extremely versatile and good on everything, tahini, in our (literal) book, is a mother sauce. Served right away before cooling, it's definitely more sauce-like, but as it cools in the fridge, it thickens up to a proper dip consistency. Either way, it's heaven, whether alone or with the volume turned up. We've included a handful of enhanced tahini recipes for you, so ready the crudités and sound the sandwich alarm!

Classic Tahini Sauce

MAKES 2 CUPS

Tahini isn't really something you'd want to eat straight from a jar—it's a little intense. Add water and the texture totally changes to a lush, creamy sauce. Give it a little salt, lemon, and garlic, and the result is a classic tahini sauce (or dip, or spread, or whatever you want to call it).

See photo on page 114.

1 cup tahini
1 garlic clove, grated on a Microplane
¼ cup lemon juice (about 2 lemons)
2 teaspoons kosher salt

1   Before measuring, stir the tahini (as you would with separated peanut butter), making sure it's homogeneous. Add to a medium bowl along with the garlic, lemon juice, and salt and whisk to combine.

2   Slowly add ⅔ cup water[1] to the tahini mixture, whisking vigorously[2] until the mixture is completely smooth and lightly aerated.

3   Refrigerate for up to 5 days.

1
You might need more or less water to get to your desired consistency. Good rule of thumb: Go slow. You can always add more water, but it's much harder to correct having added too much.

2
As you pour the water in, the tahini will get very stiff at first. As you keep going, it will start to thin again.

Go Green Tahini

To make an herby tahini sauce, follow the Classic Tahini Sauce (opposite) instructions, but before adding the ⅔ cup water, puree it in a high-powered blender with 2 cups of herbs. Any combination of soft herbs like basil, dill, parsley, and cilantro is great. You want mostly leaves, though a little stem is fine. Other green things, like spinach or arugula, also work. Use what you've got, but try to include at least a little basil if you can—it really sings.

Kale Tahini with Pomegranate Molasses

A killer party dip, this one's always a crowd-pleaser. It's peanut-butter-and-jelly–like, but the eat-your-greens version. There's no measurement on the pomegranate molasses, so you get to decide how much is the right amount. But! The right amount is more than you think.

1 leek, white and light-green parts only, halved lengthwise then cut crosswise into ¼-inch half-moons

2 bunches lacinato (Tuscan) kale, stems removed, leaves torn into 2- to 3-inch pieces

¼ cup olive oil

1 bay leaf

3 teaspoons kosher salt

2 cups Classic Tahini Sauce (page 116)

Pomegranate molasses,[1] for serving

1   In a medium bowl, cover the sliced leeks with cold water and agitate to release any trapped dirt between the leek layers. Lift the leeks from the water, draining well. Wash the torn kale in the same manner and set aside.

2   In a large pot, combine the olive oil, leeks, bay leaf, and 1 teaspoon of the salt. Cover the pot and cook the leeks over medium heat for 5 minutes, stirring occasionally.

3   Add the kale, remaining 2 teaspoons salt, and ¼ cup water. Cover with a lid for 1 to 2 minutes to partially wilt the kale. Uncover the pot and continue cooking, stirring occasionally, until the kale is soft, about 15 more minutes. Remove the bay leaf and let the veg cool to room temp.

4   Transfer the mixture to a food processor and pulse for 10 seconds. Scrape down the sides with a rubber spatula and pulse for 5 more seconds to break down the kale into small bits.[2] Add the tahini sauce and pulse to combine, scraping down the sides as needed.

5   Refrigerate for up to 5 days. To serve, transfer to a bowl and top with a generous glug of pomegranate molasses.

1
If you can't (or simply don't want to) find pomegranate molasses, a syrupy balsamic or saba would do.

2
If your kale struggles to spin in the food processor, adding a tablespoon or so of water will help move things along.

Tahini with Honeyed Kumquat + Cardamom

Top a bowl of tahini sauce with this mixture, and you have a snazzy, salty-sweet dip. (Tahini aside, don't stop yourself from spooning this honeyed citrus topping over some vanilla ice cream.)

Get Ahead
The honeyed kumquat topping can be stored in the fridge for up to 1 week.

2 tablespoons sesame seeds

2 tablespoons honey

1 tablespoon white wine vinegar

1 cup kumquats,[1] quartered and seeded, or thinly sliced into rounds

⅛ teaspoon ground cardamom

Pinch of kosher salt

⅛ teaspoon orange blossom water

2 cups Classic Tahini Sauce (page 116)

1 Preheat the oven to 300°F. Line a baking sheet with parchment paper.

2 Spread the sesame seeds on the lined baking sheet and toast for 15 minutes. Remove from the oven and set aside.

3 In a small saucepan, combine the honey, vinegar, kumquats, cardamom, and salt. Cook over low heat to reduce the liquid until it's lightly syrupy,[2] about 10 minutes.

4 Remove from the heat. Stir in the orange blossom water and sesame seeds, then let cool to room temperature.

5 Spoon over the tahini sauce to serve.

1
If kumquats are hard to come by, you could easily use mandarin orange segments, or even grapefruit. Just wait to add your citrus segments until the liquid has reduced.

2
It can be tricky to tell when your perfect reduction moment has arrived. You should be able to run a spoon through the liquid and see a trail in its wake that fills back in pretty quickly. If no trail remains, keep reducing. If the liquid is slow to fill the gap, you should add a spoonful of water to loosen it up. We like a thin maple syrup consistency rather than a thick honey consistency here.

Tahini with Green Olives + Calabrian Chile

This is a spicy little number, and perhaps our favorite tahini topper of all. It should be quite punchy and would be a kick in the pants to any deli sandwich.

Get Ahead
The marinated olives can be stored in the fridge for up to 1 week. Let come to room temperature, about 30 minutes, to melt the oil before tossing with the parsley.

1 cup pitted green olives, such as Castelvetrano, coarsely chopped
¼ cup olive oil
1 bay leaf
2 teaspoons coriander seeds, coarsely ground in a spice grinder or mortar and pestle
2 garlic cloves, grated on a Microplane
2 tablespoons jarred Calabrian chiles,[1] chopped
Grated zest of ½ orange
3 tablespoons orange juice
2 tablespoons red wine vinegar
½ cup parsley leaves
2 cups Classic Tahini Sauce (page 116)

1   Place the olives in a small heatproof bowl.

2   In a small saucepan, combine the olive oil, bay leaf, coriander, and garlic. Cook over low heat, stirring frequently, until the garlic begins to sizzle, about 5 minutes.

3   Add the Calabrian chiles and orange zest and cook for 2 to 3 minutes longer, stirring occasionally.

4   Stir in the orange juice and vinegar and pour the mixture over the olives. Remove the bay leaf and let cool.

5   To serve, fold in the parsley leaves and spoon on top of the tahini sauce.

1
If you have trouble finding a jar of Calabrian chiles, sub in a teaspoon or two of chile flakes.

Toasted Fennel Seed Tzatziki

The only difference between a run-of-the-mill tzatziki (delicious) and this one is the fennel seed. And what a difference a seed makes. Tzatziki is one of the most iconic dips the world over, but it's also versatile as a sandwich spread or as a mayo stand-in for a yogurt-y version of a chicken or tuna salad. Dip, spread, or salad, this tzatziki is the major sauce upgrade you've been searching for.

Get Ahead
Holds great for 3 or 4 days.

2 cups labneh, store-bought or homemade (page 98)
2 Persian (mini) cucumbers, grated on the largest holes of a box grater
1 garlic clove, grated on a Microplane
1 tablespoon fennel seeds,[1] toasted and ground
1½ teaspoons kosher salt
2 tablespoons olive oil

1   In a medium bowl, combine the labneh, grated cucumbers (and cucumber liquid,[2] if using store-bought labneh), garlic, toasted fennel, salt, and olive oil. Stir together until fully incorporated.

2   Store in the fridge[3] until ready to enjoy!

---

[1]
If using whole fennel seeds, toast in a small skillet over medium-low heat until fragrant, then cool and whir them in a spice grinder or pound them in a mortar. If using ground fennel, use the same amount and toast it lightly in a nonstick pan until fragrant and lightly browned.

[2]
If you're using the Kismet Labneh (page 98), omit the cucumber liquid, since our labneh is thinner than store-bought.

[3]
This dip tastes better once the flavors have gotten a chance to know one another, an hour or two.

Smoky Fish Dip

This good-for-all-seasons spread is the starter you're going to be making for any and every gathering. The tarragon-and-chile-flake topping whispers, "This is no basic fish dip." For a party, serve your smoky spread with potato chips. If you manage to squirrel some dip away, your morning bagel will be blessed.

½ cup plain whole-milk yogurt (not Greek)

1 cup full-fat sour cream

Grated zest of 1 lemon

1 tablespoon lemon juice (about ½ lemon)

1 teaspoon onion powder

½ teaspoon kosher salt

3 ounces smoked trout, picked from skin
    and bones (¾ cup)

2 ounces trout roe (optional)

¼ cup tarragon leaves, chopped

1 tablespoon Marash or Aleppo pepper[1]

1   In a medium bowl, combine the yogurt, sour cream, lemon zest, lemon juice, onion powder, salt, and smoked trout and mix together. If using the trout roe, fold it in (or dollop it on top just before serving for more drama).

2   Transfer the dip to a serving dish (if serving later, keep it in the fridge until ready to serve).

3   In a small bowl, lightly toss together the chopped tarragon and pepper flakes. Top the dip with the mixture and serve.

[1]
There's a wide world of chiles out there that you can't buy preground. Guajillos, in particular, make a nice substitute here. Just lightly toast the whole chiles in a hot pan with a little oil, then grind them in a food processor.

Garlicky Bean Dip

A garlicky bean dip is hard to beat. Topped with brown buttery black olives, consider this the undefeated champ of the creamy bean world. Something to know about us is that we almost always throw a cinnamon stick into a pot of beans, and this is no exception. It may not be the first flavor that comes to mind when conjuring up dreams of beans, but we guarantee the sweet thrill of cinnamon will win you over.

Beans
1 cup dried white beans (like butter
    or cannellini)
½ cup olive oil
½ Spanish onion, root intact
½ cup garlic cloves (about 1 head), smashed
1 bay leaf
1 cinnamon stick

Olive Topping
3 tablespoons unsalted butter
2 sprigs rosemary, cut into thirds
¼ cup oil-cured Moroccan olives,
    pitted and torn
1 tablespoon lemon juice (about ½ lemon)

To Finish
1 teaspoon kosher salt
Freshly ground black pepper

1 **Prepare the beans:** Soak the beans in 4 times their volume of cold water overnight. Drain.

2 Add the olive oil, onion (cut-side down), and smashed garlic to a large heavy-bottomed pot. Set over medium heat and cook until the onion and garlic have browned, 5 to 8 minutes.

3 Add the bay leaf, cinnamon stick, drained beans, and 5 cups water. Increase the heat to high and bring to a boil. Reduce to a simmer and cook until tender, about 1 hour.

4 **Meanwhile, make the olive topping:** In a small saucepan, combine the butter and rosemary. Cook over medium heat until frothy, 2 to 3 minutes. Reduce the heat to low, swirling occasionally until the butter browns,[1] 5 to 10 more minutes. Remove from the heat and stir in the olives and lemon juice.[2] Set aside.

5 Once the beans are tender, discard the onion, bay leaf, and cinnamon stick. Reserving the cooking liquid, drain the beans. Measure out 1 cup of the cooking liquid.

6 **To finish:** Transfer the cooked beans to a food processor, add the salt, and run until smooth, 1 to 2 minutes. Add a bit of the cooking liquid, if need be (otherwise discard the excess liquid).

7 Spoon the warm bean dip into a serving dish. Spoon the olives over the bean dip, top with a few cracks of freshly ground black pepper, and serve.

1
Don't be afraid to really brown your butter. You want its signature deep, nutty flavor. Push it a little further than you think.

2
Feel free to leave the rosemary stems in there. They should be crisped up and make a fun and tasty garnish.

Pickley Cheesy Greens

Maybe our next book will be a lavish volume of steakhouse sides. Why do we love the genre so much!? Steak is great, sure, but the sides are what we really show up for. We've riffed on the theme here and present a deeply indulgent greens dip with a tinge of tang. Serve it as a side (to steak or anything at all) or as an epic snack for chip dipping.

Get Ahead
You can make the spinach dip, minus the panko topping, a day or two ahead and store it in the fridge until ready to bake. Heat the dip in the oven without the panko until hot all the way through, then add the topping and bake according to the recipe.

¼ cup plus ¼ teaspoon kosher salt
12 cups spinach,[1] about 4 large bunches
½ bunch dill, stems included
½ bunch parsley, stems included
¼ teaspoon freshly ground black pepper
4 scallions, sliced into small rounds
1 cup full-fat sour cream
8 ounces cream cheese, at room temperature
1 cup grated white cheddar cheese
1 cup half-moon slices dill pickles[2]
½ cup panko bread crumbs
2 tablespoons olive oil
1 garlic clove, grated on a Microplane

1   Preheat the oven to 350°F.

2   In a large pot, combine 8 cups water with ¼ cup of the kosher salt and bring to a boil.

3   Working in batches, blanch the spinach and herbs with their stems until tender—30 seconds for the spinach, 3 to 5 minutes for the dill and parsley.

4   Drain the veg in a colander and, when cool enough, use your hands to thoroughly squeeze out all of the liquid. Roughly chop the cooked greens.

5   In a large bowl, combine the cooked greens with the remaining ¼ teaspoon salt, the pepper, scallions, sour cream, cream cheese, and cheddar and mix well. Add the pickles and mix to distribute. Transfer to a small (such as a 6-inch square) broilerproof dish.[3]

6   In a small bowl, combine the panko, olive oil, and grated garlic and mix to evenly distribute. Sprinkle the panko mixture over the top of the greens.

7   Bake for 20 minutes. Set the oven to broil and broil until nicely browned on top, about 5 minutes.

[1]
You can use any greens or herbs you like. (We think the flavor of the dill is pretty crucial, so maybe don't omit it.) You're looking for 3 cups total of cooked, squeezed-out greens.

[2]
A spicy dill pickle would be a fun way to go here, too. Or even a pickled jalapeño, if you're into that kind of thing. Just make sure it's not a sweet pickle.

[3]
You can skip step 6 if you don't want to bother with the bread-crumb topping. A naked spinach dip is still a spinach dip worthy of your time.

Main Event Veg

We're always happy to have a meal made up of a vegetable or two, a sauce, some rice or bread, and call it a day! We've never been ones to subscribe to the notion that animal protein ought to be at the center of the plate. We really like that lots of people choose to eat this way at our restaurants, too, regardless of whether they eat meat. Making vegetables taste delicious and feel substantial does not need to take a lot of work, but it does help to have a few solid recipes up your sleeve.

"Fried" Cauliflower with Caper Yogurt

This is one of our most iconic Kismet dishes. It's been on the menu since day one (and was, in fact, a Glasserie dish before that). It's a testament to the fact that sometimes the simplest ideas are the best ideas.

At the restaurant, you'd better believe we deep-fry to our hearts' content, but frying at home can be a heavy lift. So much oil, so much splatter, and oil disposal—it's . . . a lot. So we've given you the gift of roasting, a great alternative to the deep-fry. That said, if you're game to fry, fry on.

Get Ahead

The caper yogurt holds for several days in the fridge. Feel free to get a jump on it.

1 head cauliflower, cut into large florets (about 8 cups)
¼ cup plus 2 tablespoons olive oil
4½ teaspoons kosher salt
1½ cups drained full-fat Greek yogurt
1 garlic clove, grated on a Microplane
¼ teaspoon freshly ground black pepper
⅓ cup chopped capers
1 teaspoon sumac
¼ cup tarragon leaves

1 Preheat the oven to 475°F.

2 On a baking sheet, coat the cauliflower florets with ¼ cup of the olive oil and sprinkle evenly with 1½ teaspoons of the salt. Roast until you get deep caramelization on the edges that touch the pan, 20 to 30 minutes, flipping halfway through if needed.

3 In a small bowl, stir together the yogurt, grated garlic, pepper, capers, and remaining 2 tablespoons olive oil and 3 teaspoons salt. Stir to fully combine. Refrigerate until ready to serve.

4 On a serving plate, dust the cauliflower with the sumac and top with the tarragon. Serve with a hefty dollop (or all) of the caper yogurt.

Tangy Toasty Sweet Potatoes

Many versions of peanut-topped veg have graced the Kismet menu over the years, but these sweet potatoes are a particular favorite. The combination of roasty, sticky sweet potatoes and tangy-sweet, garlicky peanuts is one of the finer earthly delights. Nuttier than their yellow counterparts, brown mustard seeds are a surprising little something to add to this celebration of peanuts, not to mention a fun opportunity to show off your pantry's deep pockets!

Get Ahead

You can make the peanuts a day or two ahead. Just stash them in the fridge and rewarm them before spooning them over your sweeties.

Peanuts

1 cup peanuts[1]
3 tablespoons unsalted butter
1 teaspoon brown mustard seeds
2 garlic cloves, grated on a Microplane
2 teaspoons Aleppo
2 tablespoons olive oil
½ teaspoon kosher salt
3 tablespoons pomegranate molasses

Sweet Potatoes

4 to 6 sweet potatoes, depending on size
3 tablespoons olive oil
2 teaspoons kosher salt

To Finish

Flaky sea salt (such as Maldon)
¼ cup dill leaves
½ cup cilantro leaves

1 **Make the peanuts:** Preheat the oven to 275°F.

2 Spread the peanuts on a baking sheet and toast for 40 minutes. When cool enough to handle, coarsely chop them.

3 Leave the oven on and increase the oven temperature to 400°F.

4 In a small saucepan, heat the butter over medium-low heat, swirling often until it foams and then browns, 4 to 5 minutes. Add the mustard seeds, grated garlic, and Aleppo and swirl together for 20 to 30 seconds. Stir in the chopped toasted peanuts, olive oil, salt, and pomegranate molasses. Remove from the heat.

5 **Cook the sweet potatoes:** Arrange the sweet potatoes on a baking sheet, prick them with a fork, and coat evenly in 1 tablespoon of the olive oil and 1 teaspoon of the salt. Pour ¼ cup water into the pan, cover with foil, and seal tightly.[2] Roast until tender all the way through, about 45 minutes. Remove the foil and let cool.

6 Halve the sweet potatoes lengthwise. Sprinkle the cut sides with the remaining 1 teaspoon salt.

7 Heat a cast-iron griddle or skillet over medium-low heat. Add the remaining 2 tablespoons olive oil, followed by the sweet potatoes, cut-side down. Brown for 10 to 12 minutes, pressing down lightly with a spatula for even caramelization.

8 **To finish:** Transfer to a plate and top with the peanut mixture, flaky salt, dill, and cilantro.

1
Alternatively, skip the toasting step and buy roasted peanuts. We won't knock Planters. If you buy salted peanuts, omit the flaky sea salt at the end.

2
The pricking and the water both work to help the skin stay tender and stick to the potato.

Buttered Turnips
with Preserved Lemon

Turnips are tragically underrated. This dish is the evolution of one of our favorite snacks (which, while on the Kismet menu, even garnered the high praise of Jonathan Gold): raw white turnips with good butter and chopped preserved lemon—a little ode to the timeless classic, radishes with butter. And if you've never tried a Tokyo (or Hakurei) turnip, you should get your hands on some, stat. A superstar farm in the greater LA area, The Garden Of, grows the best turnips on the planet. Creamy and sweet, you could bite into one and almost mistake it for a piece of fruit.

These simple turnips would make a great addition to any brunch spread, finding themselves right at home next to some seedy bread, a fresh cheese, and a couple of soft-cooked eggs.

2 bunches white turnips[1]
2 tablespoons unsalted butter
1 tablespoon olive oil
1 bay leaf
1½ teaspoons kosher salt
1 tablespoon chopped preserved lemon rind
½ teaspoon dried mint
¼ teaspoon Aleppo
1 tablespoon lemon juice

1 Trim the turnips to leave 2 inches of stem and cut the turnips in half. Slice the greens into 2-inch pieces. Set the greens aside.

2 In a large sauté pan, melt the butter with the olive oil and bay leaf over medium-low heat. Add the turnip halves, salt, and preserved lemon and give it a stir. Sauté gently, stirring often, until almost fork-tender, about 20 minutes.

3 Sprinkle in the dried mint and Aleppo and cook for 2 to 3 minutes more.

4 Discard the bay leaf and stir in the lemon juice. Toss in the reserved turnip greens to wilt,[2] stirring for another minute or two. Remove from the heat and serve.

1
Small white turnips not only should be easy enough to find at a farmers' market but are also often tucked into groups of colorful radishes at the grocery store. You can go with a mix of turnips and radishes, if that's what you can find.

2
You can cover the pan for an even quicker wilt.

Peppered Honeynut Squash

Much like the best outfits, this deceptively simple-looking dish is going to make you work to look so casual. The challenge here mostly entails sourcing five different kinds of peppercorns.

Neal Winterbotham, Kismet's longtime sous-chef, calls this blend of many peppers "pepper force," and now so do we. Whole peppercorns are the ticket here (and preground pink or green peppercorns are basically impossible to find, anyway). If you can't find all of the various peppercorns, no big deal. You can sub the same amount of any of the other ones.

We've included a quick parsley salad to spoon over the squash, but if you happen to know how to track down some lovage (an herb that tastes like celery leaf), we would lovage to encourage that.

Get Ahead
Both the pepper force and the apple honey hold for ages. Store the pepper force in an airtight container; cover the apple honey and keep it in the fridge. Make them whenever, and try not to use them all up elsewhere before making this dish.

Pepper Force

1¼ teaspoons pink peppercorns
1 teaspoon green peppercorns
¾ teaspoon black peppercorns
½ teaspoon white peppercorns
¼ teaspoon Sichuan peppercorns

Squash

2 Honeynut or 1 small butternut squash, halved lengthwise and seeded
2 tablespoons olive oil
1 teaspoon kosher salt
4 garlic cloves, peeled
4 sprigs thyme
4 bay leaves, cut in half

Apple Honey

1 cup apple cider (or organic apple juice)
2 tablespoons apple cider vinegar
2 teaspoons honey
½ teaspoon kosher salt

Parsley Salad

1 cup parsley leaves
¼ teaspoon kosher salt
½ teaspoon olive oil
½ teaspoon lemon juice

1 **Make the pepper force:** In a spice grinder, peppermill, or using a mortar and pestle, crack the peppercorns to a coarse consistency. Set aside.

2 **Bake the squash:** Preheat the oven to 350°F.

3 Set the squash halves cut-side up on a baking sheet. Brush with the olive oil and sprinkle with the salt. Evenly divide the garlic, thyme, and bay leaves among the squash halves, tucking them into the cavities where the seeds were removed.

4 Pour ½ cup water[1] on the bottom of the pan and cover tightly with foil. Bake the squash until knife-tender, 45 minutes to 1 hour. Discard the garlic, thyme sprigs, and bay leaves.

5 **Meanwhile, make the apple honey:** In a small saucepan, heat the apple cider over medium heat and reduce until syrupy (you're looking for a similar consistency to thin honey), 20 to 25 minutes.

6 Stir in the vinegar, honey, and salt and simmer 2 to 3 minutes longer.

7 When the squash is done, set the broiler to high. Spoon the apple honey over the cooked squash and broil, rotating occasionally, until the surfaces of the squash are well caramelized but not burnt, 7 to 8 minutes.

8 Remove from the broiler and generously dust the surface of the honeyed squash with a layer of pepper force. Add ¼ cup water to the bottom of the pan and broil for 5 to 6 minutes longer, rotating occasionally, until the surfaces of the squash are well caramelized but not burnt.

9 **Meanwhile, toss together the parsley salad:** Roughly chop the parsley. In a small bowl, toss the parsley with the salt, olive oil, and lemon juice and massage the parsley a bit to break it down. Let sit until ready to serve.

10 Spoon the parsley salad over each squash and serve.

[1] The water will help to steam the squash, resulting in more tenderness. Ideally, the skin will be edible, too.

Moroccan-Spiced Carrots

We've had some version of this dish kicking around the Kismet menu since opening, and there's a reason we just can't quit it: Carrot Spice. There's nothing it's not good on. Chicken: Yes. Shrimp: Genius. Popcorn: Sure, why not!? You can make three to four times this amount and have it around for anything and everything. Here, we throw Carrot Spice in with (appropriately) carrots, which make a pretty perfect meal, paired with rice and labneh.

Get Ahead

You can cook the chickpeas up to 3 days ahead. In fact, they tend to taste better when they've had at least a night to soak up all of the flavor from the cooking liquid.

Chickpeas

½ cup dried chickpeas[1]
1 tablespoon plus ¼ cup olive oil
3 garlic cloves, smashed and peeled
½ onion, root intact
½ cinnamon stick
1 bay leaf
1 tablespoon kosher salt

Carrots

2 pounds carrots, scrubbed, halved
    lengthwise and then crosswise
¼ cup olive oil
2 teaspoons kosher salt

To Finish

4 tablespoons unsalted butter
⅓ cup minced shallots (about 2 shallots)
2 tablespoons[2] Carrot Spice (recipe follows)
2 tablespoons lemon juice (about 1 lemon)
1 cup (about ½ bunch) cilantro leaves

1   **Cook the chickpeas:** Soak the chickpeas in at least four times their volume of cold water overnight. Drain.

2   In a large heavy-bottomed saucepan or Dutch oven, heat 1 tablespoon of the olive oil over medium-high heat. Add the garlic and onion and brown for 3 to 4 minutes. Add the cinnamon, bay leaf, drained chickpeas, 3 cups water, and remaining ¼ cup olive oil. Bring to a boil, then reduce to a simmer, cover, and cook until the chickpeas are creamy all the way through, 1 to 1½ hours.

3   Discard the onion, cinnamon, and bay leaf. Stir in the salt and allow to sit uncovered, off the heat, for at least 30 minutes. When ready to use, drain the chickpeas of their liquid.[3]

4   **Roast the carrots:** Preheat the oven to 450°F.

5   Arrange the carrots on a baking sheet and toss in the olive oil and salt to coat. Roast the carrots until tender and browned at the edges, 30 to 40 minutes, stirring halfway through.

6   **To finish:** About 10 minutes before the carrots have finished roasting, melt the butter in a sauté pan over medium heat. Add the chickpeas and sauté until the butter browns lightly, about 10 minutes. Add the shallots and cook, stirring for 3 minutes longer. Add the Carrot Spice and stir thoroughly.

7   Pour the spiced chickpeas over the carrots on the baking sheet, add the lemon juice, and toss well.

8   Transfer to a serving dish and top with the cilantro.

Carrot Spice

MAKES ½ CUP

In a small bowl, whisk together the Marash pepper, coriander, cumin, paprika, turmeric, black pepper, and cinnamon. Store in an airtight container.

Carrot Spice

3 tablespoons Marash or Aleppo pepper
3 tablespoons ground coriander
1½ teaspoons ground cumin
1½ teaspoons ground paprika
1½ teaspoons ground turmeric
1½ teaspoons ground black pepper
1½ teaspoons ground cinnamon

1

In a pinch, you can sub in a can of chickpeas here, but cooking your own chickpeas will always be better.

2

We're down to use more of the Carrot Spice here, but if you're a little spice-cautious, start with just the 2 tablespoons. You can always dust a bit more on at the end.

3

Save the chickpea cooking liquid! Whether in the fridge or frozen for the future, it's a flavorful base for braises or a quick soup.

Stewy Cranberry Beans + Greens

Canned beans can be handy in a pinch, but cooking your own beans from dried is irrefutably the way to go. You can infuse them with flavor throughout the cooking process—whereas with canned beans, you're starting with a flavor deficit. Once you get in the habit of cooking your own beans, you'll understand our devotion. It's also worth noting that beans, in general, tend to be even better the second day, after a good long mellow.

Once these beans have had a night to get to know their aromatics, we spice them up with a can-do-no-wrong bean spice blend and wilt in some greens. At Kismet, we use fermented turnip greens as an alternative to the Swiss chard called for here. If you're into fermentation and you have some store-bought kraut, kimchi, or Chinese fermented mustard greens hanging around, we definitely suggest adding in or subbing one of those in to add some lactic tang to these beans.

Bean Spice [1]

¼ cup olive oil
3 dried arbol chiles,[2] stemmed
3 dried guajillo chiles, broken and seeded
2 garlic cloves, chopped
1 teaspoon ground coriander
1½ teaspoons ground fennel
½ teaspoon Aleppo
¼ teaspoon ground cardamom
¼ teaspoon freshly ground black pepper

Beans

½ cup olive oil
5 garlic cloves, smashed
½ onion, halved lengthwise, root intact
½ cinnamon stick
1 bay leaf
1½ cups dried cranberry beans,[3] soaked in
    at least four times their volume of cold
    water overnight, and drained
1 tablespoon kosher salt

To Finish

4 cups Swiss chard (about 1 bunch),
    stems finely chopped and leaves
    roughly chopped
1 garlic clove, grated on a Microplane
2 tablespoons lemon juice (about 1 lemon)

1. **Make the bean spice:** In a skillet, heat the olive oil over medium-low heat. Add all of the chiles and toast, stirring frequently for 3 to 4 minutes. Transfer the chiles to a plate and let cool.

2. Using the oil that's already in the pan, reduce the heat to low, add the chopped garlic, and cook, stirring, until lightly browned, 3 to 4 minutes. Add the coriander, fennel, Aleppo, cardamom, and black pepper. Remove from the heat and stir to lightly toast the spices in the residual heat of the hot pan. Set aside.

3. Transfer the cooled chiles to a blender and whir into small pieces, 30 to 60 seconds, scraping down as needed. Transfer the ground chiles to a small bowl, and stir together with the toasted spice mixture. Set the bean spice aside.

4. **Cook the beans:** In a large heavy-bottomed saucepan, heat the olive oil over medium-high heat. Add the smashed garlic and onion and brown for 3 to 4 minutes. Add the cinnamon, bay leaf, drained beans, and 5 cups water. Bring to a boil, then reduce to a simmer, cover, and cook until the beans are creamy all the way through, about 45 minutes. Turn off the heat, and discard the onion, cinnamon, and bay leaf. Stir in the salt and let sit for 20 minutes.

5. **To finish:** Stir the bean spice into the cooked beans. Stir in the Swiss chard, return the pot to medium heat, and cook for 3 to 4 minutes to wilt the greens. Once wilted, add the grated garlic and lemon juice, and serve.

1
Bean spice, a simple version of a chile crisp, is also just Anything Spice because it's, ya know, good in anything. For example, toss with tomatoes for a quick tomato-cilantro salad, or mix a spoonful into thick yogurt for a quick dip.

2
If you don't have whole dried arbol or guajillo chiles, use whatever whole dried chiles you have, or even sub in a mix of sweet and hot dried chile powder.

3
Cranberry beans are also known as borlotti beans. If you can't find them, pintos or even a white bean, such as cannellini, would make a decent sub here.

Grilled Corn in Pepperoncini Butter

The grilled-corn equivalent of a salt-and-vinegar chip, this recipe hits that perfect-for-a-summer-day sweet spot. We like cutting our corn into smaller pieces here because they're easier to rub around in the vinegary pool of butter. You could also cut the kernels from the cob and toss with the butter for a warm salad version, or keep your ears whole if you can't be bothered. (We'll take any excuse to use those little pronged, corn-shaped corn-grabber things.) But no matter how you cut the corn, make sure you spoon a generous amount of the pepperoncini butter over it and continue to dip as you make your way through—you want that hit of spice and sour in every bite.

Pepperoncini Butter

1 stick (4 ounces) unsalted butter

4 garlic cloves, grated on a Microplane

1 teaspoon kosher salt

¼ teaspoon ground white pepper

½ cup thinly sliced pepperoncini[1]

1 tablespoon pepperoncini pickling liquid

Corn

4 ears corn, husked, each ear cut into
    4 equal pieces[2]

¼ cup neutral oil, such as canola
    or sunflower

1 teaspoon kosher salt

1 **Make the pepperoncini butter:** In a small saucepan, combine the butter and garlic and cook over medium heat until the butter turns golden brown and the garlic is toasty, 7 to 10 minutes. Remove from the heat, stir in the salt, white pepper, sliced pepperoncini, and the pickling liquid. Set aside.[3]

2 **Grill the corn:** Preheat a grill to medium-high heat.

3 In a large bowl, coat the corn with the oil and sprinkle with the salt. Grill the corn for 8 to 12 minutes, turning frequently to lightly char all sides.

4 Transfer the grilled corn to a serving dish, spoon the pepperoncini butter over, and serve.

1
Presliced pepperoncini do exist, but we want you to buy them whole and slice them as thin as you can here. They'll stick better to the corn that way.

2
To cut the corn, use a big knife, even a cleaver. It helps to go a little hard on the first strike and then keep the knife in the corn and bang the whole thing into the cutting board to break it apart. It's a little dramatic but a nifty trick for cutting through tough things (winter squash in particular).

3
If your butter solidifies as it sits while you're grilling the corn, just warm it a bit before using.

Beans on Beans

What's better than beans? The answer: more beans. Here, we give you the fine duo of grilled green beans and canned butter beans in a creamy tahini vinaigrette—a keep-it-simple, beans-on-beans dish. It makes a happy addition to a potluck or holiday, and it definitely delivers as a satisfyingly quick weeknight meal, paired with an egg and a piece of toast. If you're feeling ambitious, you could very easily add even more beans and really run with the prompt. Romano beans, chickpeas, fresh favas, peas—you simply cannot go wrong pairing beans with more beans.

Tahini Vinaigrette

½ cup tahini

2 teaspoons honey

1 tablespoon kosher salt

½ garlic clove, grated on a Microplane

¼ cup white wine vinegar

1 (15-ounce) can butter beans,
    drained and rinsed

Grilled Green Beans

1½ pounds green beans

2 tablespoons neutral oil,
    such as canola or sunflower

1 teaspoon kosher salt

2 tablespoons olive oil

1 **Make the tahini vinaigrette:** In a medium bowl, whisk together the tahini, honey, salt, and grated garlic. Add ⅓ cup water and the vinegar and whisk until smooth. Toss in the butter beans and, using a spoon, gently stir into the vinaigrette.

2 **Grill the green beans:** Preheat a grill, grill pan, or cast-iron griddle to medium-high.

3 In a bowl, toss the green beans with the neutral oil and salt. Grill/griddle them until lightly charred, about 5 minutes. (If cooking on a grill, use a grill basket, or even a wide mesh metal sieve, so the beans don't fall through the grates, tossing frequently.)

4 Transfer the cooked beans to a serving dish and spoon the beany tahini vinaigrette over the top. Top with the olive oil and serve.

Caraway Cabbage Gratin

We often opt for a lighter take on cabbage, but a gratin cannot be denied. A deeply indulgent way to eat your vegetables, this could make even the most carnivorous among us swoon. And about the blue cheese: Well, it may have found its highest calling here as an indispensable purveyor of richness and funk.

1 head cabbage (about 2½ pounds),
    cut into 8 or 10 wedges
3 tablespoons olive oil
3 teaspoons kosher salt
2 cups heavy cream
¾ cup diced shallots (2 or 3 shallots)
1 sprig thyme
1½ teaspoons ground caraway
¼ teaspoon freshly ground black pepper
½ cup crumbled blue cheese, such
    as Gorgonzola

1   Preheat the oven to 450°F.

2   Arrange the cabbage wedges on a baking sheet. Coat the cabbage evenly with the olive oil and sprinkle with 2 teaspoons of the salt. Roast until deeply browned, about 40 minutes, flipping the pieces over halfway through. Remove from the oven.

3   Leave the oven on and reduce the temperature to 400°F.

4   Meanwhile, in a small saucepan, combine the cream, shallots, thyme, 1 teaspoon of the caraway, the black pepper, and remaining 1 teaspoon salt. Bring to a simmer (being careful not to let it boil), then reduce the heat to medium-low and cook for 6 minutes to infuse the flavors into the cream. Remove from the heat and discard the thyme sprig.

5   In a large baking dish, arrange the cabbage wedges in a single layer.[1] Pour the shallot cream over the top, distributing evenly over the cabbage. Sprinkle the blue cheese crumbles over the top (especially in the divots between cabbage pieces), and dust with the remaining ½ teaspoon caraway.

6   Bake for 25 minutes. As this gets close to being done, the edges should start to look nicely caramelized, and the cream's bubbles will start to slow in speed.[2]

7   Remove from the oven and let sit for 15 minutes before serving.[3]

1
While not essential, snipping through the core holding each wedge together will make it easier to serve (and eat) later.

2
Be careful not to push it too far as you'll run the risk of breaking the cream.

3
You want the molten lava that is gratin to cool to a palatable temperature.

Gingery Glazed Onions

We have yet to meet a human who doesn't love a tender little onion. These onions are adapted from one of our all-time favorite condiments: the jammy, gingery onions that adorn the Chicken Pita at Rotisserie, an ode to the very '90s curried chicken salads of our youth. This style of glazed onion often leans a little sweet by our standards, so we've tempered that with a splash of tangy yogurt and brought in a little life via some peppery arugula. The result is an ideal center stage veg dish.

Get Ahead

You can make the onions a day or three in advance and store them in the fridge. Just heat them back up when you're ready to serve them, then top with the yogurt and arugula. If you want to go the extra mile, wait to add the ginger juice until you reheat them to keep the flavor punchy.

1½ pounds unpeeled cipollini onions

2 tablespoons olive oil

1¼ teaspoons kosher salt

1 tablespoon unsalted butter

1 sprig thyme

2 teaspoons honey

2 tablespoons apple cider vinegar

1 teaspoon ground turmeric

⅓ cup plain whole-milk yogurt

½ garlic clove, grated on a Microplane

2 tablespoons golden raisins

2 tablespoons ginger juice[1]

1½ cups arugula (about ½ bunch)

1   Bring a medium pot of water to a boil. Add the cipollini onions and blanch[2] for 30 seconds. Drain in a colander, run them under cold water, and let sit for a minute to fully drain. When cool enough to handle, using a paring knife, cut the top end of each onion (opposite the root), so they're flat on the top. Trim the root side down just a bit, but keep the root intact (to hold the onion together), and peel the skin away.

2   In a large sauté pan with a lid, heat the olive oil over medium heat. Add the onions in a single layer, flat-side down. Sprinkle 1 teaspoon of the salt evenly over them and brown for 5 minutes, swirling occasionally for even cooking. Flip the onions and add the butter, thyme, honey, vinegar, turmeric, and 1 cup water. Agitate the pan in a circular motion to evenly combine the sauce, making sure the onions end up in a single flat layer. Cover, reduce the heat to medium-low, and simmer the onions for about 30 minutes, until tender.

3   While the onions are cooking, in a small bowl, whisk together the yogurt, grated garlic, and remaining ¼ teaspoon salt. Set the yogurt sauce aside.

4   Once the onions are tender all the way through,[3] remove the lid and add the golden raisins. Continue simmering uncovered until the liquid is reduced to a light syrup consistency, another 10 to 15 minutes.

5   Just before serving, stir in the ginger juice. Transfer to a shallow bowl. Spoon the yogurt sauce over the onions, top with the arugula, and serve.

1
To get 2 tablespoons ginger juice, start with about a 2-inch piece of ginger. Grate it on a Microplane and press in a fine-mesh sieve set over a bowl to catch the juice.

2
Blanching is a quick trick that majorly cuts down the cipo peeling time. You can skip it if you'd prefer to peel them the old-fashioned way.

3
Using a paring knife, pierce the tops of the onions gently to test for tenderness. They're ready when they put up no fight.

Perfect Smashed Potatoes

Simmer-smash-crisp, the holy trinity of root vegetable cooking techniques, never fails to deliver. It strikes the ideal balance of soft interior and crunchy exterior—the texture dreams are made of and the ultimate crowd-pleaser. At times, we've topped these with a few swipes of dry-cured scallop, and if you, too, feel inclined toward a fishy flourish, bottarga (or even trout roe or caviar) would make a lovely stand-in, but it's fully optional. It's also worth noting that what we have here is yet another example where the finishing touch of raw garlic makes a good dish a little extra good.

2 pounds small potatoes, such as fingerlings
     or new potatoes
2 bay leaves
3 tablespoons kosher salt
⅓ cup olive oil
1 tablespoon Urfa pepper
1 garlic clove, grated on a Microplane
1 cup labneh, store-bought or homemade
    (page 98)
Grated zest of ½ lemon
⅓ cup dill leaves
½ teaspoon flaky sea salt

1   In a large pot, combine 6 cups water, the potatoes, bay leaves, and salt and bring to a boil over high heat. Reduce to a simmer and cook until the potatoes are fork-tender, 30 to 40 minutes.[1] Once tender, drain the potatoes well and transfer to a baking sheet.

2   Preheat the oven to 450°F.

3   Toss the potatoes with the olive oil and, using the back of a metal spatula, lightly smash the potatoes. Roast until the potatoes are very nicely crisped, about 45 minutes, occasionally tossing for even browning. Remove the pan from the oven, sprinkle the potatoes with the Urfa and grated garlic, and toss to coat evenly.

4   Spread the labneh over the bottom of a serving dish and pile the dressed potatoes over it. Top with the lemon zest, dill, and flaky salt.

1
Potato cooking time can vary widely with different potatoes. Start checking them at 20 minutes.

Salt to Taste

"Salt to taste" is a second-nature phrase for anyone who cooks regularly. To us, it's self-explanatory and as obvious as "just make it taste good." That said, we do recognize how such an ambiguous direction might be tricky, and "to taste" could seem to mean anything. While we've avoided it throughout these pages in an effort to be precise, we think "salt to taste" is worth a mention because we want you to trust your tongue, both with these recipes and in general.

While these recipes were tested, it doesn't mean that every condition will be the same for you as for us. Vegetables and fruits vary widely in their water and sugar content, proteins can be slightly bigger or smaller, and other seemingly small details can throw off any recipe's precise measurements. You should think of a recipe generally as a guideline and use your active judgment to achieve the best result. We will always advise you to trust your taste over the exact amount written on the page. And if something tastes like it wants a touch more salt, pinch away!

Cooking is all about practice, and like any creative endeavor, the more you do it, the more you'll deepen your relationship to it and get a handle on seasoning. Restaurants are notorious for heavy seasoning ("seasoning," in restaurant-speak, typically just means salt). And while some people find that restaurants go a little too far (and sometimes they do), very often restaurant cooking is particularly delicious because of the liberal use of salt. We never want anything to taste salty, but we do know that properly seasoned food requires more salt than most home cooks think. If you're unsure, that's okay! Just go slow and taste along the way.

Fun with Fritto

Fried things—especially battered-and-fried things—want to be eaten right away, which makes them a particularly good choice for a mingle-y snack hour before a dinner party. Anytime you decide to fry, you should get comfortable being glued to the stove while people enjoy the fried fruits of your labor. It's all part of the fun: frying in rounds, finishing a plate followed by another, sneaking a snack yourself between batches.

Depending upon the season, you could use any number of other veggies in this recipe (asparagus, steamed kabocha, or oyster mushrooms, for some options). But we insist on keeping the lemons—they bring a surprisingly indispensable zing to their fried friends.

¼ cup rice flour

½ cup cornstarch

1 cup chickpea flour

1 teaspoon baking powder

2 teaspoons kosher salt

¾ cup sparkling water, ice cold[1]

6 cups neutral oil, such as sunflower or canola

3 medium zucchini, cut into 4-inch-long crudités-style spears

1 lemon, sliced into thin rounds, seeds removed

1 red onion, cut into 12 wedges

½ cup plain whole-milk yogurt (not Greek)

¼ cup honey

1 teaspoon Aleppo

1 teaspoon fennel pollen[2]

1 teaspoon flaky sea salt

1 In a medium bowl, whisk together the rice flour, cornstarch, chickpea flour, baking powder, and salt. Gradually whisk in the sparkling water to form a batter. (You may not need to add all of the water. Go slow so as not to thin it too much—you're looking for something resembling pancake batter.)

2 Pour the oil into a heavy-bottomed medium pot (it should reach about 4 inches up the sides of the pot) and heat the oil to 350°F. Line a tray with paper towels.

3 Working in batches, submerge the zucchini, lemon, and onion pieces in the batter to coat them evenly. Using a pair of tongs, chopsticks, or even a slotted spoon, pull the veg from the batter, allowing a little (but not all) of the excess batter to fall from the pieces before transferring them to the oil.

4 Carefully drop the battered pieces in batches, one at a time, into the hot oil, being mindful not to overcrowd the pot.[3] Fry until crisp, about 1½ minutes, and remove using a slotted spoon or spider. Drain on the paper towels.

5 Transfer the pieces to a serving dish and top with the yogurt and honey. Dust with the Aleppo, fennel pollen, and flaky salt, and dig in.

[1]
Very cold sparkling water is important for texture. Throw your already cold can (or bottle) into the freezer for 15 minutes to get it extra chilly before using.

[2]
Toasted ground fennel seed is a perfectly good alternative to fennel pollen.

[3]
Aside from not wanting to overcrowd, which will cause the pieces to stick to one another, an important reason to fry in batches is to maintain the oil temperature. If it drops too low, you'll have oil-logged batter, and the end result won't feel as light and crispy.

Seafood

Seafood: What's not to love? It always feels like a treat. Plus, it cooks quickly, making it a cinch to slap together a luxurious meal. We're partial to shellfish, in particular, because it's so interactive! We love a lengthy eating experience with lots of digging, shelling, and dipping. And for as much as we adore shellfish, sometimes you cannot beat a simply cooked piece of fish. This section gives you a little bit of both because you just don't have to choose.

Dressed-Up Tinned Fish

I remember when tinned fish first caught my eye. I was perusing the canned tuna aisle of a grocery store in Tulsa, Oklahoma, when I was touring the country as a teenage musical theater performer, and I noticed something: a can of sardines packed in oil. Bones and all, the line of little stacked soldiers was a revelation. Living out of hotel rooms—where a kitchen starts and stops with the coffee maker—would make anyone develop an affinity for the marvel that is precooked protein. It was the beginning of a lifelong love affair.

In recent years, tinned fish options have exploded, a serious improvement from the early days of one decent variety of sardine. You have plenty of choices in the world of tinned fish, but for this easy dish, I might suggest mackerel above all. Top it with a stylish garnish, like these pickled green tomatoes, and you'll seem like you've done way more than open a can. —Sara Kramer

¼ cup hazelnuts

3 small green tomatoes,[1] thinly sliced on a mandoline (about 1 cup)

2 tablespoons distilled white vinegar

½ teaspoon coriander seeds

2 teaspoons sugar

2 teaspoons kosher salt

1 tablespoon lime juice (about 1 lime)

2 (4-ounce) tins fish packed in olive oil, ideally mackerel, but sardines work, too

Flaky sea salt

½ cup parsley leaves

1 Preheat the oven to 275°F.

2 Spread the hazelnuts on a small baking sheet and toast for 30 minutes. Let cool, then coarsely chop.

3 Place the sliced green tomatoes in a small heatproof bowl.

4 In a small pot, combine the vinegar, ¼ cup water, the coriander, sugar, and salt and bring to a boil. Remove from the heat and pour the hot liquid over the tomatoes. Mix in the lime juice and let cool to room temp.

5 Pull the tinned fish from the oil in its can and arrange on a serving plate. Sprinkle with flaky sea salt.

6 In a small bowl, combine the parsley, hazelnuts, a spoonful of the oil from the tin, and a spoonful of the pickling liquid from the tomatoes. Toss to coat.

7 Top the fish with the pickled green tomatoes, followed by the dressed parsley, and serve.

[1]
Green tomatoes can be a little tricky to find. Talk to farmers who sell tomatoes at your farmers' market, or pick a few unripe ones off your own vines if you garden. A firm, underripe red tomato will do just fine as well, but green tomatoes are worth seeking out and great for more than frying!

Crab Rice–Stuffed Peppers

A large stuffed pepper can be a bit much, but a mini? It's the perfect amount of pepper. The lunchbox pepper—essentially a tiny bell pepper—makes the ideal vessel. It's giving jalapeño-popper kitsch, and who wouldn't love the convenient built-in handle (the stem). Lunchbox peppers' popularity has soared in recent years beyond farmers' markets; we've started spotting them in little plastic bag bundles in grocery stores where they might be billed as "mini sweet peppers," and we're happy to see their proliferation. The crab rice stuffing brings a little extra fun to these petite peps.

Get Ahead
These hold well, covered, in the fridge for a day or two. Pull them 30 or so minutes before serving to take the chill off — they're best at room temp.

1 pound lunchbox peppers
¼ cup plus 2 tablespoons olive oil
3 tablespoons plus 2 teaspoons kosher salt[1]
½ cup short-grain or medium-grain rice, rinsed
1 cup minced shallots (about 3 shallots)
6 ounces crabmeat (about ¾ cup), picked through[2]
½ teaspoon thyme leaves, chopped
¼ teaspoon ground cloves
½ teaspoon ground allspice
Grated zest of 2 limes
3 tablespoons lime juice (about 2 limes)
1 tablespoon fish sauce

1 Preheat the oven to 350°F.

2 Cut a slit in each pepper, top to bottom, keeping the stems on and intact. On a baking sheet, toss the peppers with 2 tablespoons of the olive oil and 1 teaspoon of the salt. Roast until soft, about 15 minutes. Remove from the oven and let cool.

3 In a large pot, bring 8 cups water and 3 tablespoons of the salt to a boil. Reduce to a simmer and add the rice. Cook, uncovered, until the rice is fully soft,[3] about 20 minutes.

4 Meanwhile, in a small saucepan, combine the shallots, remaining ¼ cup olive oil, and remaining 1 teaspoon salt and cook over medium-low heat, stirring occasionally, until fully soft, about 10 minutes. Transfer to a medium bowl and set aside.

5 When the rice is cooked, drain in a sieve (as you would drain pasta). Add the rice to the shallot mixture and stir to combine. Transfer to the fridge to cool, about 30 minutes.

6 Once the rice mixture is cool to the touch, add the crab, thyme, cloves, allspice, lime zest, lime juice, and fish sauce. Mix well to fully distribute.

7 Using a spoon, overstuff the crab-rice mixture into each pepper.

1
If using a kosher salt brand other than Diamond Crystal, reduce the salt level by about one-third.

2
Run your fingers through the crabmeat to make sure there are no hidden bits of shell or cartilage.

3
We prefer slightly overcooked rice here. As this is a stuffing, it'll hold together better if it's a bit on the mushy side.

Saffron-Scented Squid
+ Broccolini

Great for a midweek meal or a potluck, this quick-cooking squid salad hits a lot of satisfying notes. Saffron and pine nuts bring a little fragrant pizzazz, while grilling the broccolini balances all of that ethereal aroma with a dose of earthy char and smoke. Grilling is definitely the optimal cooking method, but a hard roast in a cast-iron skillet is a solid alternative.

2 tablespoons pine nuts

Vinaigrette
A pinch of saffron, crumbled by rubbing
    between your fingers
¼ cup lemon juice (about 2 lemons)
2 teaspoons kosher salt
1 red chile, such as a Fresno, sliced into
    thin rounds
½ garlic clove, grated on a Microplane
3 tablespoons olive oil

Squid + Broccolini
1 pound cleaned squid, bodies and
    tentacles separated
3 bunches broccolini, ends trimmed
4 tablespoons olive oil
3½ teaspoons kosher salt
1 cup basil leaves

1 Preheat the oven to 275°F.

2 On a baking sheet, toast the pine nuts until golden, about 20 minutes. Let cool and coarsely chop.

3 **Make the vinaigrette:** In a large bowl, combine the saffron, lemon juice, salt, sliced chile, and garlic and let marinate for 5 minutes. Whisk in the olive oil and set aside.

4 **Grill the squid and broccolini:** Preheat a grill to high.

5 Spread the squid out onto paper towels to dry it.

6 Toss the broccolini with 3 tablespoons of the olive oil and 1½ teaspoons of the salt. Grill the broccolini[1] until lightly charred and tender, 6 to 10 minutes. Set aside and, once cool enough to handle, cut into big bite-size pieces.

7 Toss the squid with the remaining 1 tablespoon olive oil and 2 teaspoons salt. Grill the squid[2] over high heat for 1 to 3 minutes, depending upon the size, flipping with tongs once or twice. You'll know the squid are done when they change color fully from milky to stark white. Once cooked, slice the bodies into ½-inch rings. If the tentacles are bigger than bite size, cut in halves or quarters.

8 Add the grilled broccolini, squid, and pine nuts to the bowl with the saffron vinaigrette and thoroughly toss. Finish with the basil and serve.

1
If your broccolini is on the larger side, try splashing (or spraying) it with some water to help steam it while it grills (or cover it with a metal bowl or tray for a similar effect).

2
If your squid are particularly small, consider a grill basket or putting a cast-iron skillet or flattop griddle directly onto your grill so they don't slip through the grates.

An Unintimidating Whole Fish

We genuinely couldn't think of a whole fish recipe we'd want to include more than this one: a branzino, butterflied and broiled, dusted in sumac and served with a generous portion of aioli. We did think through countless alternatives, though. We love a whole grilled fish, but grilling without sticking to the grates is tricky. Few things in life are better than a whole fried fish, but frying at home is a messy endeavor. We wanted—here it is— an unintimidating whole fish. Pair it with a few radishes and an herby salad and pretend you're seaside.

Get Ahead
Make the aioli up to 3 days ahead. The garlic flavor may soften a bit.

Aioli

⅓ cup canola oil
⅓ cup olive oil
1 large egg
2 tablespoons lemon juice (about 1 lemon)
2 garlic cloves, grated on a Microplane
1 teaspoon kosher salt

Branzino

1 whole branzino (1½ pounds), butterflied[1]
2 teaspoons olive oil
1 teaspoon kosher salt
1 teaspoon sumac (optional)

1 **Make the aioli:** In a liquid measuring cup, combine the canola and olive oils. Separately, in a tall container, combine the egg, lemon juice, garlic, and salt and use a stick blender to blend them together. Slowly stream in the oil, keeping the head of the blender low in the container, until all of the oil has emulsified. Store in the fridge.

2 **Cook the branzino:** Set the broiler to high. On a baking sheet, rub the fish evenly with the olive oil and sprinkle the salt on both sides.

3 With the skin-side up, broil until just cooked through, about 6 minutes. (It will continue to cook just a bit more as it sits.) Remove from the broiler, let sit for a minute, and dust with sumac, if using.

4 Transfer to a platter and serve with the aioli.

[1]
You should ask your fishmonger to butterfly the branzino, but if the only option is whole, you can use kitchen shears for a rough alternative. Clip out the spine by starting from the underside and cutting down through the middle, alongside either side of the spine, unburying and removing it carefully. In either case, keep an eye out for small bones when eating.

Cozy Risotto with Mussels

Risotto is so much less tricky than people seem to think. Yes, it requires constant stirring (both to develop its classic creamy porridge vibe and to cook the grains evenly), but in the end, it's really very forgiving because even slightly overcooked risotto is still very satisfying. Here, a silky, squash-y, easier-than-you-expected risotto gets topped with another simple step-up: bright mussels steamed in white wine and cream. It's the perfect dead-of-winter upgrade from either a lonely risotto or a solo pot of steamed mussels.

Risotto

¼ cup olive oil

2 cups diced yellow onion (about 1 onion)

1 bay leaf

2½ teaspoons kosher salt

¼ teaspoon freshly ground black pepper

6 garlic cloves, grated on a Microplane

½ small butternut squash,
    peeled and grated (2 cups)

1½ cups Arborio rice

1 cup white wine

1 teaspoon fennel pollen[1]

1 tablespoon fish sauce

Mussels

2 tablespoons white wine

Grated zest of 3 lemons

1 bay leaf

2 pounds mussels, scrubbed

⅔ cup heavy cream

½ teaspoon kosher salt

For Serving

⅓ cup parsley leaves

1 lemon, quartered

Olive oil, for finish

1 **Make the risotto:** In a large heavy-bottomed pot, combine the olive oil, onion, bay leaf, salt, and pepper. Cook, stirring occasionally, over medium heat for 15 minutes to lightly caramelize the onion.

2 Add the garlic and cook for 10 more minutes, continuing to stir often. Add the squash and cook for 5 minutes to soften, stirring occasionally.

3 Stir the rice into the squash, followed by the white wine, and cook for 5 minutes to evaporate the wine. About one cup at a time, add 4½ cups water, stirring constantly. Wait until the previous cup of water has mostly been absorbed before you add the next cup. Cook until all of the water is added and the rice is cooked and creamy, 15 to 20 minutes total. Finish by stirring in the fennel pollen and fish sauce.

4 **Steam the mussels:** Meanwhile, when the rice is almost cooked, in a large pot, combine the white wine, lemon zest, and bay leaf and bring to a boil over medium-high heat. Add the mussels, cover, and steam for 2 to 3 minutes. Once all of the mussels have opened, swirl in the heavy cream and salt.

5 **To serve:** Plate the risotto in four individual bowls, spooning the mussels over the top. Finish with the parsley, a lemon wedge, and a touch of olive oil.

1
If you don't have fennel pollen, you can sub in ground fennel seed, preferably toasted.

Maybe Your Clam Isn't Dead (and Other Tips for Cooking Shellfish)

• When you pull clams out of your fridge, you might notice that some of them are open. While this does sometimes mean they are dead, it's not always the case. If you give them a few taps, they might close right up, very much alive. If they don't, they are indeed dead and should be thrown away.

• We don't want bits of mud or sand stuck to the outsides, so be sure to give your shellfish a good scrub under running water.

• Before you cook mussels or clams, they need to be "purged" to get rid of any sand trapped inside the shells. Cover them in water with lots of kosher salt in it, and set the uncovered bowl back in the fridge. Purging attempts to mimic their preferred environment: cold, salty water. After an hour or two, they will begin to open up, releasing any sand that they have inside. The sand will sink to the bottom of the bowl, so be sure to lift (not dump) them out.

• There is a common misconception that when a clam or mussel doesn't open as fast as the others in the pot that it is dead. In fact, sometimes these are the most alive, muscles clenched, holding their shells closed longer than the rest. Don't give up on them so fast! Often when given a few more minutes, they will pop right open.

• When cooking mussels, make sure the meat comes away from the shell completely before removing them from the pan. It should be very easy to pick a mussel from its shell; an undercooked mussel will be quite difficult, both to remove from the shell and to eat.

Clams + Peas "au Poivre"

Steak au poivre is one of those canonical dishes for a reason: Its depth of flavor defies its true simplicity. We wanted to bring that same feeling of luxurious ease to a pot of clams, and we added a little springtime with peas. As with all things easy, the devil's in the details. No one likes a sandy clam, so be sure you have enough time to soak them clean. Beyond that, the biggest trick here is timing: Don't overcook anything, and you'll have 'em raving about your clams and peas for years to come.

1 cup minced shallots (3 or 4 shallots)
1 bay leaf
3 tablespoons olive oil
1½ teaspoons kosher salt
1½ teaspoons coarsely ground black pepper
½ cup Cognac or other brandy
3 pounds clams, such as littlenecks, purged[1]
      and scrubbed
2 cups crème fraîche
2 cups peas (fresh or frozen)
Grated zest of ½ lemon
1 teaspoon lemon juice

1   In a large pot with a lid, combine the shallots, bay leaf, olive oil, salt, and pepper and cook over medium heat until the shallots are softened, 3 to 5 minutes.

2   Pour in the Cognac and reduce until almost fully evaporated, 3 to 5 minutes.

3   Add the clams and ¼ cup water, increase the heat to high, and cover. Keep an eye on the clams[2] and, as they begin to pop open—3 to 5 minutes—remove them from the pot to a nearby large bowl.

4   When all of the clams have opened—7 to 10 minutes—and are in the bowl, stir the crème fraîche into the pot and cook for 3 to 5 minutes to thicken the broth slightly.

5   Stir in the peas and cook for 1 minute. Return the clams to the pot and toss. Finish with the lemon zest and juice and serve immediately.

1
For how to "purge" clams, see opposite page.

2
Different clams open at different speeds, so pay attention, lifting the lid every 15-ish seconds to check on them.

The Only Way to Bake a Salmon

Baked salmon holds a nostalgic key to my heart. Most weekends growing up, my family would unwrap wax-papered parcels of fish from Zabar's, the Upper West Side's holy land of Jewish appetizing shops. And every Yom Kippur break fast involved the full spread: fluffy cream cheese, smoked whitefish, sliced tomatoes, juicy Greek olives, and whatever outlier succeeded in catching my mother's eye—like a welcome but out-of-place ball of burrata.

Maybe it's sacrilege to prefer it to peppered lox (the Kramer house favorite), but lightly smoky baked salmon has always been the one for me. I pile it on buttered toast, give it a squeeze of lemon, and swoon. This soft and supple version bears very little resemblance to the many *other* baked salmons of my youth. Listen, I never turned down the broiled, Soy Vey–smothered salmon we ate for Shabbat dinner (that's every Friday night for those of you unfamiliar— yes indeed, every single Friday). But who knew that lowering the oven temp makes all the difference in the world?

This low-and-slow method is *the* way to bake a salmon—a little more time to dedicate, sure, but barely. Plus this salmon dish shines at any temp; it's just as much a star set out cold for breakfast as it is served straight from the oven for dinner. Paired with Almond "Aioli" (page 109), it's the stuff of dreams.

—Sara Kramer

½ red onion
1½ teaspoons paprika
1½ teaspoons kosher salt
1 garlic clove, grated on a Microplane
½ teaspoon ground caraway
½ teaspoon ground coriander
½ teaspoon Aleppo
Grated zest of ¼ orange
2 tablespoons olive oil
1½- to 2-pound salmon fillet
2 oranges, peel cut away, sliced into thin
     rounds, seeds removed
1 tablespoon rice vinegar
½ cup dill leaves

1   Preheat the oven to 250°F.

2   Slice the onion into thin rounds and soak in cold water for 10 minutes. Pull from the water, drain well, pat with paper towels, and set aside.

3   In a small bowl, combine the paprika, 1 teaspoon of the salt, the garlic, caraway, coriander, Aleppo, orange zest, and 1 tablespoon of the olive oil.

4   Place the salmon, skin-side down, onto a baking sheet, and rub the top evenly with the spice mixture. Let it sit for 15 minutes.

5   Transfer to the oven and bake until just cooked through, 40 to 45 minutes.[1]

6   In a medium bowl, combine the red onion, orange rounds, vinegar, the remaining 1 tablespoon olive oil and ½ teaspoon salt and toss. Top with the dill.

7   Transfer the salmon to a serving plate and spoon the orange/ onion mixture alongside.

[1]
Two ways to help you know when your salmon is done: 1. The color changes from dark to light when cooked – the center will cook through last. 2. When you press (gently) on the salmon, it should visibly flake from the pressure. Err on the side of undercooking – you can always pop it back in.

Blistered Shishitos + Shrimp

This recipe is a bit of a curveball. Rose and sage? Not the likeliest of aromatic acquaintances for shishitos and shrimp. Turns out, lucky for all of us, it's a surprisingly supernatural combination and, better still, a breeze to throw together. Earthy and saline, floral and vegetal, rich and bright: This fragrant dish hits all the notes and wants a hunk of good bread by its side.

1 tablespoon olive oil
½ pound shishito peppers
2 teaspoons kosher salt
1 stick (4 ounces) unsalted butter
10 sage leaves
6 garlic cloves, smashed
1 tablespoon dried rose petals[1]
2 teaspoons Aleppo
1 pound shrimp, peeled and deveined
¼ teaspoon rose water
2 tablespoons lemon juice (about ½ lemon)

1   In a large cast-iron skillet, heat the olive oil over medium-high heat. When it begins to shimmer, add the shishito peppers and sprinkle with 1 teaspoon of the salt. Blister for 3 to 5 minutes, tossing occasionally. Remove from the heat and set the peppers aside on a plate.

2   Return the skillet to low heat. Add the butter, sage, garlic, rose petals, and Aleppo. Cook, stirring occasionally, until the garlic is lightly browned, 7 to 10 minutes.

3   Increase the heat to medium, toss in the shrimp, sprinkle with the remaining 1 teaspoon salt, and sauté, stirring, until they are no longer translucent, 3 to 4 minutes.

4   Turn off the heat, return the shishitos to the pan, along with the rose water and lemon juice, and stir to combine. Serve hot.

1
Look to a spice store for rose petals, or order from Kalustyan's (they ship!). If all you have is rose water, this dish will still be delicious without the petals.

Halibut Skewers with Tomatoes + Coconut Vinaigrette

The dressing in this salad is inspired by one of our favorite Vietnamese noodle dishes, bánh tằm bì, which gets bathed in a rich-yet-light coconut vinaigrette. The basis of this dream-sauce is coconut cream. A workhorse of an ingredient, coconut cream adds dairy-free depth to anything from braises to sweets. It's the ideal consistency for this satisfying and wildly simple sauce, which we toss with cherry tomatoes and spoon over fragrant spice-flecked halibut skewers. No skewers? No problem. Keep your halibut in fillets and add a minute or two to the cook time.

1½ pounds skinless halibut, cut into about 1-inch cubes

3 teaspoons kosher salt

1 tablespoon ground cardamom

2 teaspoons ground green peppercorns[1]

5 tablespoons olive oil

2 bay leaves

¼ cup coconut cream[2]

2 teaspoons lemon juice (about ½ lemon)

2 cups cherry tomatoes, halved

½ cup mint leaves

1 In a medium bowl, sprinkle the halibut with 2 teaspoons of the salt, the cardamom, and ground green peppercorns. Toss to coat evenly. Add 2 tablespoons of the olive oil and toss to coat again. Let marinate for at least 30 minutes (but no more than 2 hours) in the fridge.

2 Meanwhile, in a small saucepan, combine 2 tablespoons of the olive oil with the bay leaves and warm over low heat, swirling occasionally, for 2 to 3 minutes.

3 Discard the bay leaves and pour the bay-infused oil into a small bowl. Stir in the coconut cream, lemon juice, and remaining 1 teaspoon salt. Set the coconut vinaigrette aside.

4 Thread 4 or 5 pieces of halibut onto a skewer,[3] repeating for a total of 8 skewers. Hold in the fridge, covered, until ready to cook.

5 Preheat a cast-iron skillet or griddle over medium-high heat. Add the remaining 1 tablespoon of olive oil to the pan and sear the skewers, being careful not to break them as you flip them, until they are no longer translucent, 30 to 60 seconds per side, 3 to 4 minutes total. Transfer the cooked skewers to a serving dish.

6 Toss the cherry tomatoes with the coconut vinaigrette and spoon over the skewers. Top with the mint and serve.

---

[1] Green peppercorns are unripe black peppercorns. They're more herbaceous and fruity, and you can find them at a specialty spice shop or order them online. We recommend getting dried peppercorns, not the kind packed in vinegar. If you don't have them, any other type of peppercorn will do!

[2] Coconut cream is key here. It's much thicker than coconut milk. Be careful not to get the sweetened version.

[3] Ideally, you're using flat skewers — the delicate fish will be less likely to want to break off of them.

Broiled Bass with Chorizo + Kale

Greens, meat, and fish: This recipe is a one-stop shop. This seemingly simple gal has a little more going on under the surface, though, thanks to the tamarind concentrate, a specialty ingredient you're going to want to keep on hand to swirl into yogurt or to perk up a marinade. Here, it brings a deep tang to earthy kale, spicy chorizo, and flaky striped bass. If you can't find striped bass, any white-fleshed, skin-on fish will do.

1 pound striped bass, cut into 4 equal
    portions
2 tablespoons olive oil
3 teaspoons kosher salt
2 links fresh chorizo (about ¾ pound),
    casings removed
5 garlic cloves, sliced
1 bunch scallions, cut into 2-inch pieces,
    white and green parts kept separate
¼ cup tamarind concentrate
1 tablespoon tomato paste
1 teaspoon Aleppo
3 bunches kale, stems removed and
    leaves torn
2 tablespoons lemon juice (about 1 lemon)

1. Coat the bass pieces with 1 tablespoon of the olive oil and sprinkle with 1 teaspoon of the salt. Set aside.

2. Preheat the broiler to high.

3. In a large broilerproof skillet, heat the remaining 1 tablespoon olive oil over medium heat. Crumble in the chorizo, lightly browning it for 5 to 7 minutes. Remove it from the pan and set aside. Add the garlic and scallion whites to the hot pan and cook, stirring occasionally, until lightly browned, 1 to 2 minutes.

4. Stir in 1 cup water, the tamarind, tomato paste, Aleppo, and the remaining 2 teaspoons salt. Bring to a simmer, then wilt in the kale in two batches, covering in between.

5. Return the chorizo to the pan, along with the scallion greens, and mix into the kale to distribute. Nestle the fish into the pan, skin-side up, pushing it down into the liquid.

6. Broil until the fish is cooked through, 7 to 9 minutes. Squeeze on the lemon juice before serving.

Eggy + Meaty

For all our talk of vegetables, we do actually love meat. We opened a rotisserie chicken restaurant, after all—we're clearly devoted. We don't always want meat to be the star of the show, but when we do, we want it to shine. And let's not forget eggs; they hardly need an introduction, as one of the world's most perfect foods.

Kismet Kuku with Big Beans

Kukus, frittatas, and Spanish tortillas are all in the family of set-and-slice egg dishes, which make the perfect breakfast or lunch option when you're cooking for a crowd. They're done ahead of time, delicious at any temperature, and deceivingly impressive. This eggy slice of heaven is inspired by a classic Persian kuku, essentially an herby, greens-packed frittata, just bound by egg. This version involves greens, too, but the addition of beans and cream makes it a definite departure from tradition.

We originally developed this dish using barberries, the teeny dried fruit also called zereshk (you should be able to find them in a Middle Eastern specialty store), which provide a zap of tang between bites of custardy egg. We've subbed in dried cranberries here because they're similarly tart and much easier to find, but they can also be omitted entirely if you're trying to have less fun. Do you not like fun?!

Get Ahead

Feel free to cook the beans and/or make the kuku cream a day or two ahead. Store in the fridge until ready to party. Bring to room temp before combining with the eggs.

Beans

¾ cup dried butter (or gigante or lima) beans[1]
¼ cup olive oil
½ yellow onion, quartered, root intact
1 bay leaf
½ cinnamon stick
1½ teaspoons kosher salt

Kuku Cream

1 shallot, thinly sliced
1 cup heavy cream
2 teaspoons kosher salt
1 bay leaf
1 sprig thyme

Kuku

7 large eggs, at room temperature[2]
1 cup frozen chopped spinach,[3] thawed and
    squeezed of any excess water
2 tablespoons dried cranberries,
    roughly chopped
2 teaspoons olive oil

1. **Prepare the beans:** Soak the beans in at least four times their volume of cold water overnight. Drain.

2. In a medium pot, heat the olive oil over medium-high heat. Add the onion and cook until it begins to brown, about 5 minutes. Add the bay leaf and cinnamon stick. Cook for 30 seconds, then add the soaked beans and 6 cups water. Bring to a boil, then reduce the heat to medium-low and simmer until the beans are tender, 1 to 1½ hours.

3. Discard the onion, bay leaf, and cinnamon. Stir in the salt and allow the beans to sit off the heat for at least 1 hour. Drain off the liquid and set the beans aside.

4. **Make the kuku cream:** In a medium saucepan, combine the shallot, cream, salt, bay leaf, and thyme and bring to a light simmer over medium-low heat. Cook until reduced by one-third of the total volume, about 15 minutes. Watch closely to not let it boil over. Once reduced, discard the thyme and bay leaf. Set the cream aside.

5. **Make the kuku:** Preheat the oven to 350°F.

6. In a large bowl, whisk the eggs. Add the kuku cream, cooked beans, the spinach, and cranberries. Stir to combine.

7. In a 10-inch, well-seasoned cast-iron or ovenproof nonstick skillet, heat the olive oil over medium heat, swirling the pan to coat the bottom and sides evenly, 3 to 4 minutes.

8. Transfer the egg mixture to the skillet using a rubber spatula to evenly spread out the kuku contents. Transfer the skillet to the oven and bake until just set, about 30 minutes.

9. Allow the kuku to cool in the pan for at least 15 minutes, before turning out onto a cutting board or serving dish. Flip over to the presentation side, slice, and serve.

1
You could also skip the bean soaking and cooking and use 1½ cups canned beans instead. Add ½ teaspoon salt to the drained canned beans and let them sit for at least 20 minutes before using.

2
Bringing your eggs up to room temp cuts down the amount of total cooking time, which we like.

3
Frozen spinach is a time-saver here, but this is also a good way to use up any mix of old greens you have in the fridge. You just want to end up with about 1 packed cup of cooked, squeezed-out greens.

EGGY + MEATY

Breakfast-Lunch-Dinner Soup

This marriage of several good soups (think avgolemono meets egg drop meets minestrone) is one of the likeliest meeting points of our two home cooking styles. We both love summer squash, live on broth, and cook some version of this soup at home very often. As the title suggests, this soup is great across all meals—we particularly like it for breakfast. If you happen to have a few spoonfuls of leftover rice, adding it would make this a slightly more substantial lunch or dinner.

3 cups ¼-inch-thick half-moon slices leeks, white parts only (3 or 4 leeks)

¼ cup olive oil

1 tablespoon plus 2 teaspoons kosher salt

1 bay leaf

8 cups chicken stock[1]

1 Parmesan rind,[2] 2 to 3 inches

5 cups ¼-inch-thick half-moon slices zucchini (3 or 4 zucchini)

2 tablespoons lemon juice (about 1 lemon)

4 cups spinach

2 large eggs, beaten

1   In a large pot, combine the leeks, olive oil, 2 teaspoons of the salt, and the bay leaf. Cover and cook over medium-low heat, lifting the lid to stir occasionally with a wooden spoon, until the leeks are soft, about 10 minutes.

2   Add the chicken stock, remaining 1 tablespoon salt, and the Parmesan rind. Increase the heat to medium-high and bring the liquid to a boil. Reduce to medium-low and simmer for 5 minutes. Add the zucchini and simmer 2 to 3 minutes longer. Stir in the lemon juice.

3   Discard the bay leaf and Parmesan rind. Add the spinach, stirring about 10 seconds until wilted.

4   Making sure your soup is simmering, stream in the beaten eggs in a swirl pattern, giving them one light stir.[3] Turn off the heat and serve.

[1]
Be sure to buy (or, better yet, make) chicken *stock*, not broth – ideally something made with just chicken bones. To make an even better, richer stock, add some chicken feet if you can find them.

[2]
Tossing in a Parm rind adds a little umami to soups, so we always recommend purchasing a piece with a rind.

[3]
Giving the broth just one quick stir will produce the desired threadlike texture of the eggs. Understir, and you'll end up with big chunks; overstirring will turn the broth cloudy.

Freekeh "Polenta" with Poached Eggs

Freekeh is bulgur's smoky sister, and it shines in this super-simple "polenta" as a queen among porridge grains. True polenta is made with corn, but the word feels right here, too, given the pillowy, rich result. Much like its corn cousin, this polenta makes an all-star brunch dish—we pair ours with poached eggs and Green Zhoug (page 95). It's the meal equivalent of being swaddled and, sometimes, we all need a little soothing.

Freekeh "Polenta"
1 cup freekeh
1 bay leaf
1 tablespoon kosher salt
1½ cups heavy cream

1 teaspoon distilled white vinegar
4 large eggs
¼ cup Green Zhoug (page 95)

1 **Make the freekeh "polenta":** In a blender, grind the freekeh on medium speed into smaller pieces, 1 to 1½ minutes.

2 In a large Dutch oven, combine the freekeh, 5 cups water, the bay leaf, and salt and bring to a boil over medium-high heat. Reduce the heat to medium-low and let simmer for 45 minutes, stirring frequently with a wooden spoon, and scraping the bottom of the pot as you stir.

3 Add the cream and return to a simmer. Continue stirring until it is the consistency of thick porridge,[1] about 20 minutes.

4 When the polenta is ready, in a medium saucepan, bring 4 cups water to a boil. Reduce to a simmer and stir in the vinegar. Poach the eggs one at a time. First crack an egg into a small bowl, then drop it into the water. Cook for 2 to 3 minutes, until set, then remove from the water with a slotted spoon. Repeat with the remaining eggs.

5 Serve the polenta in individual bowls, each topped with a poached egg and 1 tablespoon green zhoug.

---

[1] Taste the porridge for doneness. If it still has a bite (as in, it's not fully cooked) but it's thickening up too much, add a little extra water and keep simmering. You can't overcook it, so you're just looking to make sure it's cooked fully and the right consistency.

Harissa Party Wings

I learned many things at Blue Hill, such as how to identify chickweed and turn it into a salad, the technique for making a perfect pea puree, and that one can, in fact, be asked to dice basil. But perhaps the least expected takeaways from my time there were these two realizations: (1) Crispy wings could be made in an oven (no fryer necessary). (2) Frank's RedHot is a classic for a reason.

Trevor Kunk, the chef de cuisine at Blue Hill in Manhattan during my time there, took preparing wings for a family meal more seriously than—I'm just going to say it—pretty much anything else. I can still hear him reminding the cook on the meat station to "Shake those wings!" referring to the need to periodically jostle the tray to make sure the wings got crispy all over and not just on one side. This was *very* important to Trevor, as was the fact that the wings should be absolutely covered in spicy sauce. His sauce always had a classic Frank's RedHot and butter base but with additional spices, herbs, and extra chiles (and extra, extra chiles for people like me). We ate them in the kitchen directly out of the metal mixing bowl, standing over the garbage. More than a decade later, I still can't resist a spicy wing, and we make a version of them for family meal at Kismet, though we eat them sitting down.

Like Trevor's, our recipe starts with that same tried-and-true base. Then we add spices commonly found in harissa, the North African pepper paste. —Sarah Hymanson

Get Ahead

You can make the sauce days, even weeks, in advance. Rewarm it in a saucepan, stirring, before pouring it over the wings.

6 pounds chicken wings

½ cup neutral oil, such as canola or sunflower

1 tablespoon kosher salt

1½ cups Frank's RedHot sauce

2 garlic cloves, grated on a Microplane

1 tablespoon ground coriander

1½ teaspoons ground caraway

1½ teaspoons ground cumin

1½ tablespoons Aleppo

1 tablespoon honey

1 stick (4 ounces) unsalted butter

Grated zest of 1 lemon

2 tablespoons lemon juice (about 1 lemon)

1. Preheat the oven[1] to 500°F and at the same time preheat two baking sheets on separate racks.

2. In a large bowl, toss the wings with the oil and salt to coat. Carefully remove the hot baking sheets from the oven and spread out the wings on the baking sheets.

3. Roast for 45 minutes, flipping at the 15- and 30-minute marks.

4. Meanwhile, in a small saucepan, combine the hot sauce, garlic, coriander, caraway, cumin, Aleppo, and honey. Cook over medium-low heat, stirring occasionally, for 5 minutes. Swirl in the butter, lemon zest, and lemon juice.

5. Pour the sauce over the crisped wings and toss to coat.

[1]

If you have an air fryer (which is actually just a small convection oven), here's a great time to use it instead of a hot oven, though it might require cooking the wings in several batches.

Springtime Chicken Skewers

A great way to kick off the start of barbecue season, these lively skewers pack a lot of flavor. Taking a cue (wink) from Northern Chinese barbecue, we dust the skewers in a fennel seedy spice blend when they come off the grill. The crisp asparagus-and-fennel salad is a fun contrast to the meaty, smoky skewers—perfect for a cool, late-spring evening with friends. To round out the meal, we highly recommend pairing these with the Pine Nut Pepper Schmear (page 110).

Get Ahead

The fennel sprinkle holds for up to a week in a sealed container. After that, it may start to clump.

Fennel Sprinkle

1 tablespoon ground toasted fennel seeds

¼ teaspoon kosher salt

¼ teaspoon sugar

½ teaspoon onion powder

Chicken

1½ pounds chicken thigh meat,[1] cut into 1-inch cubes

1 yellow onion, quartered

2 garlic cloves, peeled

¼ cup olive oil

2 teaspoons kosher salt

1 sprig rosemary, leaves picked and stem removed

Salad

¼ cup plus 1 teaspoon kosher salt

1 bunch asparagus, ends trimmed, cut crosswise into ¼-inch rounds

½ teaspoon honey

Grated zest of 1 lemon

2 tablespoons lemon juice (about ½ lemon)

⅓ cup olive oil

1 tablespoon capers, drained and chopped

1 bulb fennel, shaved thinly on a mandoline

¼ cup chopped fennel fronds (just the green frilly parts)

1 **Make the fennel sprinkle:** In a small bowl, combine the ground toasted fennel, salt, sugar, and onion powder. Mix to combine. Store, covered, until ready to use.

2 **Marinate the chicken:** Place the chicken pieces in a sealable container. In a blender, combine the onion, garlic, olive oil, salt, and rosemary leaves and blend on high until smooth, about 1 minute. Strain through a fine-mesh sieve into the chicken container and toss to coat. Cover and marinate in the fridge for at least 2 hours and up to overnight.

3 Load 5 pieces onto each skewer for a total of 8 skewers and stash in the fridge until ready to grill.

4 **Prep the salad:** In a medium saucepan, combine 4 cups water and ¼ cup of the salt and bring to a boil. Add the asparagus and blanch for just 5 seconds.[2] Drain in a colander and set aside.

5 In a medium bowl, combine the honey, lemon zest, lemon juice, olive oil, capers, and remaining 1 teaspoon salt. Whisk together and set the bowl of dressing aside.

6 Preheat a grill to medium-high heat.[3] Grill the skewers, turning, until cooked through, 3 to 4 minutes per side, 12 to 15 minutes total.

7 Place the cooked skewers on a platter and, using a fine-mesh sieve, dust on all sides with the fennel sprinkle. Add the shaved fennel, asparagus, and fennel fronds to the dressing bowl and toss. Spoon the salad over the dusted skewers and serve.

[1] Feel free to buy boneless, skinless thighs for ease, but you get extra points for deboning skin-on thighs and getting a little crispy skin in the mix.

[2] You want still-crisp asparagus. It doesn't need more than a dunk in boiling water.

[3] You may want to use a rag or paper towel to oil the grates before grilling to help avoid any skewer stickage.

Chicken Schnitzel
with Giardiniera

This schnitzel is about as Hymanson-Kramer as a Hymanson-Kramer collab can get—an idea so apparent that it came together in seconds, like it already existed. Chicken schnitzel with a sesame-studded crust was an ever-present staple in the Kramer house, and pickley giardiniera basically floods the streets of Chicago, Hymanson's hometown. At Kismet, the two get stacked between thick slices of brioche, along with a swipe of umami-rich "schnitzel sauce" and a fat slab of iceberg, to make a flamboyant sandwich "toothpicked" by a steak knife. While you can absolutely go the sandwich route (just add bread and lettuce), we've decided to pare back to the essentials. And while we think the sauce is "essential," we can also concede that if you want to further simplify by using labneh or yogurt (or mayo or aioli or sour cream, or any combination of any of these) instead, we'll live. You'll still have the unbeatable combination of crispy chicken, spicy pickle, and cool-creamy sauce, and you can't do much better than that.

See photo on page 195.

Get Ahead

The giardiniera holds for several weeks in the fridge, and the schnitzel sauce holds for several days. Prep both in advance and you'll have an easy-breezy schnitzel sesh on your hands.

Giardiniera

2 cups thinly sliced cauliflower
(about ½ head)
2 cups thinly sliced celery (4 or 5 stalks)
2 cups thinly sliced carrots
(about 2 large carrots)
1 cup thinly sliced Fresno chiles
(5 or 6 chiles)
3 cups distilled white vinegar
⅓ cup kosher salt
¼ cup sugar
2 cups olive oil
8 sprigs thyme
2 bay leaves
2 teaspoons Aleppo
2 teaspoons ground fennel

Schnitzel Sauce

1 egg yolk
½ teaspoon kosher salt
2 teaspoons sugar
1 garlic clove, grated on a Microplane
1½ teaspoons chopped thyme
Grated zest of 1 lemon
1 tablespoon lemon juice (about ½ lemon)
1 tablespoon distilled white vinegar
2 tablespoons fermented bean curd[1]
1 cup neutral oil, such as canola or sunflower
½ cup labneh, store-bought or homemade
(page 98)

1 **Make the giardiniera:** In a large heatproof bowl, toss together the cauliflower, celery, carrots, and chiles.

2 In a medium pot, combine the vinegar, 3 cups water, the salt, and sugar and bring to a boil. Pour the pickling liquid over the veggies, cover with plastic wrap, and let sit to pickle at least 4 hours at room temperature, or in the fridge for 24 hours (or indefinitely).

3 In a small saucepan, combine the olive oil, thyme, bay leaves, Aleppo, and ground fennel and warm over medium-low heat for 5 minutes. Remove from the heat and let steep for 20 minutes. In a fine-mesh sieve, strain the oil (discard the aromatics) into a small bowl. Cover the bowl with plastic wrap and let it sit at room temp until you're ready to dress the pickles.

4 Drain the pickles of their liquid and discard or reuse the liquid.[2] Pour the aromatic oil over the drained pickles.

5 **Make the schnitzel sauce:** In a food processor, combine the egg yolk, salt, sugar, garlic, thyme, lemon zest, lemon juice, vinegar, and fermented bean curd. Pulse to combine. With the motor running, stream in the neutral oil and stop once combined.

6 Spoon the labneh into a small bowl. Add the mixture from the food processor (starting with a small amount at first to ensure the labneh stays smooth) and fold together with a rubber spatula.

Chicken Schnitzel

2 cups all-purpose flour

3 tablespoons Diamond Crystal kosher salt
(2 tablespoons if using Morton's)

4 large eggs

3 cups panko bread crumbs

¾ cup sesame seeds

4 boneless chicken breasts, each pounded[3]
to a ¼- to ½-inch thickness

1½ cups neutral oil, such as canola
or sunflower

7   **Prepare the chicken schnitzel:** Set up a dredging station in three wide dishes: In one dish, whisk together the flour and salt. In a second dish, whisk the eggs. In the third dish, combine the panko (crushing it between your fingers a bit) and sesame seeds.

8   Bread the chicken by dipping it in the seasoned flour, shaking off the excess, and transferring it to coat in the egg. Lift the chicken from the egg wash and place it in the panko, pressing to coat.

9   In a large wide heavy-bottomed skillet, like cast-iron, heat the oil over medium-high until it's shimmering but not smoking. Working in batches—each cutlet should lie completely flat in the oil—fry the chicken, turning each piece every 3 minutes or so until golden brown on all sides, 7 to 10 minutes per cutlet.

10 Serve with the schnitzel sauce and the giardiniera.

1
Fermented bean curd (as the label will likely read) or fermented tofu is an easy ingredient to pick up at any Chinese supermarket and is one of the world's utmost umami bombs. An easy sub here is white miso.

2
You can reuse the pickle liquid to pickle new vegetables — just bring it to a boil and pour it over a new batch.

3
A good tip for pounding chicken breast (or any meat, for that matter) is to place it between two layers of plastic wrap for a little protective barrier that allows it to better take the beating.

Giardiniera: An Ode

While there is some debate about which classic Chicago "sandwich" is the best (it's a hot dog), there's no question about whether giardiniera is itself an excellent condiment. In Italian, the word has two meanings: a female gardener and also mixed pickles, which makes sense given that giardiniera is an obvious way to preserve vegetables from a garden.

While in Italy you might find a whole range of different pickled vegetables, the Chicago-style "hot mix" always includes the same items—cauliflower, celery, carrots, and hot peppers—which are first pickled in vinegar and then submerged in oil. It's a perfect condiment, spicy and filled with toothsome (but not crunchy) vegetables. Eaten in generous amounts, it almost doubles as a salad. When I was growing up in Chicago, yellow-topped jars of giardiniera were so ubiquitous at grocery stores that I hardly even saw them. It wasn't until I moved away that I realized it's kind of hard to find elsewhere.

In Chicago, giardiniera is typically diced, for easy cradling in an Italian roll, but we like to slice it thinly so that if you do choose to pile it onto a sandwich, the pickles will be less likely to fall out. There are a million places where giardiniera would make things more fun and delicious. Put a little pile next to your fried eggs at breakfast, or pack yourself a turkey-giardiniera sandwich for lunch and enjoy your little "Taste of Chicago" (inside joke for Chicagoans only).

—Sarah Hymanson

Jewish Chicken

Chicken legs braised with dried fruit and vinegar: Just the smell of it, and I'm back in my parents' apartment, under the dining room table with my brother and a friend. We're on our "second cup" of Martinelli's sparkling apple juice, restlessly waiting for the Passover meal to be served.

In Jewish tradition, you are either eating or actively avoiding eating. This was one of those actively avoiding moments, hours into the seder we hosted every year. My mother had pulled out *her* mother's floral china, and someone had picked up my great-aunt Estie from the suburbs. My father had burned a "mix CD" of requisite holiday songs so that Debbie Friedman could keep us on key while we sang "Chad Gadya," an allegorical song that involves, among other things, a cat eating a goat....

When the chicken was finally served, I'm pretty sure I didn't eat it, confident I wouldn't like it, instead subsisting entirely on matzo ball soup for the night. Little did I know how good it was: the thighs alongside jammy fruit, balanced with mellowed-but-still-tart vinegar, an ever-pleasing and ubiquitously Jewish-American combo.

Thankfully, my taste has evolved since then. But really it's only in the past few years, inspired by some old kitschy Jewish cookbooks, that I've felt moved to make this dish myself. Here is our version of "sweet-and-sour chicken," lightly sweet and perfectly tangy, with a hint of ginger and clove to round it out. —Sarah Hymanson

Get Ahead

If you need something for tomorrow, later in the week, or to bring to a potluck, this is the dish you want in your back pocket. Make up to 5 days in advance and reheat, covered, in a 300°F oven for 20 to 25 minutes.

4 chicken leg quarters (thigh and drumstick)

5 teaspoons kosher salt

2 tablespoons olive oil

2 onions, cut into 8 wedges each, root end intact

⅔ cup dried apricots[1]

½-inch piece ginger, thinly sliced into 4 to 6 pieces

½ cup white wine

¼ cup white wine vinegar

4 cups chicken stock

3 tablespoons honey

1 bay leaf

⅛ teaspoon ground cloves

¼ teaspoon freshly ground black pepper

1   Season the chicken legs with 4 teaspoons of the salt. Let sit for 20 minutes.

2   Preheat the oven to 325°F.

3   In a large skillet, heat the oil over medium-high heat. Add the chicken, skin-side down, and cook until nicely browned, 8 to 10 minutes. Remove the chicken from the pan and transfer, skin-side up, to an 8 × 11-inch baking dish.

4   Add the onions to the hot skillet and cook until browned, 3 minutes per side.

5   Transfer the onions to the baking dish alongside the chicken. Add the apricots and the sliced ginger.

6   In the hot skillet, combine the white wine, vinegar, stock, honey, bay leaf, cloves, black pepper, and the remaining 1 teaspoon salt. Bring to a strong boil and cook to reduce by half, 10 to 15 minutes.

7   Pour the liquid over the chicken. Cover with foil and bake for 30 minutes. Remove the foil and bake, uncovered, until tender, another 45 minutes.

[1]
We've opted for apricots, but prunes, figs, golden raisins, or even dried apples would all make good subs.

Roast Chicken
with Schmaltzy Potatoes

Some may say the juicy bird is the point of roasting a chicken. While we're certainly proud to call this bad boy ours, we're here to tell you the bigger prize is the crunchy, golden nuggets of schmaltz-crisped potatoes underneath. (Schmaltz, for the uninitiated, is the rich, rendered fat from the chicken, which in this case pools on the bottom of the tray as the bird roasts and makes the potatoes underneath extra tasty.) At Rotisserie, we've perfected the rather exhaustive process for schmaltzy potatoes: brining, roasting, smashing, and frying. Here, we've radically simplified the process and we can triumphantly say that we don't sacrifice an ounce of what's great about the restaurant version. For the full experience, serve with Garlic Sauce (page 108) and Chile Crisp (page 107) for dipping and dousing.

1 teaspoon ground coriander

½ teaspoon ground turmeric

2 teaspoons Aleppo

½ teaspoon brown sugar

5½ teaspoons kosher salt

1 whole chicken (3½ pounds), spatchcocked[1]

2 pounds Yukon Gold potatoes, cut into
    1½- to 2-inch bite-size pieces

½ cup neutral oil, such as sunflower or canola

1 head garlic, broken into individual cloves,
    unpeeled

3 bay leaves

6 sprigs thyme

1. In a small bowl, combine the ground coriander, turmeric, Aleppo, brown sugar, and 4 teaspoons of the salt. Mix to combine.

2. Set a wire rack into a 13 × 18-inch baking sheet and place the spatchcocked chicken on top. Sprinkle the spice blend over the bird and use your hands to rub it evenly into the chicken. Transfer the uncovered chicken on the tray to the fridge[2] for at least 4 hours and up to 24 hours.

3. When ready to roast, remove the chicken from the fridge and let it come to room temperature for 30 minutes.

4. Preheat the oven to 400°F.

5. On a second 13 ×18-inch baking sheet, toss the potatoes with the oil, garlic cloves, bay leaves, thyme, and remaining 1½ teaspoons salt. Cover tightly with foil and roast for 20 minutes. Remove from the oven and discard the foil.

6. Leave the oven on and increase the temperature to 450°F.

7. Using a metal spatula, lightly smash the potatoes against the pan, spreading them out evenly. Place the wire rack with the seasoned chicken over the potatoes.[3]

[1] Spatchcocking isn't as scary as it sounds and is, in our opinion, the best way to evenly roast a chicken. Lay the chicken breast-side down and use kitchen shears to cut down either side of the backbone, removing it (and saving it in the freezer for stock). Then flip the chicken breast-side up and press firmly down to flatten the bird.

[2] Laying the chicken skin-side up and uncovered in the fridge helps to dry out the skin, which will produce a slightly crispier roast bird in the end. If you're short on fridge space, put it in a bowl, covered, or in a resealable bag.

[3] Don't worry if the rack sits directly on the potatoes; they won't suffer.

8　Roast the chicken and potatoes until a thermometer inserted in the thickest part of the bird reads 165°F, about 40 minutes. Remove from the oven but leave the oven on.

9　Using either two kitchen towels or two pairs of kitchen tongs, carefully lift off the rack with the chicken and place onto another tray or a cutting board. Let it rest for 15 minutes.

10　Using a metal spatula, scrape the potatoes away from the bottom of the pan, redistributing and flipping the crispy sides up. Return to the oven for another 15 to 20 minutes while the chicken rests.

11　Remove the potatoes from the oven, scraping up the crispy bits, and transfer to a serving dish.

12　Using kitchen shears, cut the chicken into serving pieces: Separate the thighs from the drumsticks and cut the breasts crosswise into 2 pieces each. Plate the chicken next to the potatoes and serve.

Paprika-Roasted Chicken Thighs with Grapefruit

Grapefruit and chicken: Stick with us here, we wouldn't steer you wrong. They're not the *most* obvious of matches, but supported by buttery, spice-laced leeks, it's a most perfect union. Furthermore, it's the perfect quick and lively dinner, especially during the winter when not much else is in season. A couple leeks, some clam-shelled baby greens, a grapefruit or two, and you're in business.

6 bone-in, skin-on chicken thighs
　　(about 2½ pounds total)
1 tablespoon kosher salt
4 tablespoons unsalted butter
2 teaspoons paprika
1 teaspoon Aleppo
½ teaspoon ground allspice
2 whole star anise
¼ teaspoon freshly ground black pepper
3 or 4 leeks, white and light-green parts only,
　　halved lengthwise
2 grapefruit
4 cups tender greens (like pea shoots, tatsoi,
　　or baby spinach)

1　Preheat the oven to 350°F.

2　Place the chicken thighs on a baking sheet (13 × 18 inches) and sprinkle with the salt.

3　In a small saucepan, melt the butter over low heat. Add the paprika, Aleppo, allspice, star anise, and black pepper. Remove from the heat and let sit for 10 minutes. Discard the star anise and pour the fragrant butter over the chicken.

4　Transfer to the oven and bake for 30 minutes. Remove the pan from the oven and carefully add the leeks to the pan along with ¼ cup water, mixing into the butter and pan juices.

5　Return the pan to the oven and bake for another 30 minutes. Turn on the broiler to high, and broil until nicely browned, 4 to 5 minutes.

6　While the chicken is in the oven, supreme the grapefruits by cutting the peel and white pith away with a sharp knife, then cut the segments away from between the membranes. Squeeze the juice from the core into the bowl with the segments and discard the squeezed-out bits.

7　Remove the chicken and leeks from the oven and transfer to a serving dish. Using a metal spatula, scrape up the crispy bits from the bottom of the pan to incorporate them into the pan drippings.

8　Toss the grapefruit segments and juice into the pan drippings to coat, then add the greens, wilting them lightly as you toss them with the grapefruit.

9　Spoon the grapefruit and greens around the chicken and serve.

Lamb Skewers
with Carob Molasses

These lemony lamb skewers are good for winter nights in and summer barbecues alike. Chocolaty carob molasses may be a new addition to your pantry's shelves, but you're going to swoon for it. It comes together, along with a hit of Meyer lemon, into a glaze that gracefully balances out the earthy morsels of grilled meat. We like a lively, simple watercress salad here and think that, if you've got it in you, some Classic Tahini Sauce (page 116) and Grilled Flatbread (page 229) would be the all-star cast your lamb deserves.

Marinated Lamb

½ cup carob molasses[1]

¼ cup lemon juice, preferably Meyer lemons (about 2 lemons)

1 shallot, chopped

1 teaspoon fennel seeds

⅛ teaspoon ground cinnamon

1 whole star anise

¼ teaspoon freshly ground black pepper

1 teaspoon ground coriander

1 tablespoon plus 2 teaspoons kosher salt

3 tablespoons olive oil

1 tablespoon brown sugar

1½ pounds lamb leg meat, trimmed of sinew and cut into 1-inch[2] cubes (about 40)

Watercress Salad

1 bunch watercress

1 teaspoon lemon juice, preferably Meyer lemon

1 teaspoon olive oil

1 teaspoon sesame seeds

⅛ teaspoon kosher salt

1 lemon, cut into wedges

1 **Marinate the lamb:** In a blender, combine the carob molasses, lemon juice, shallot, fennel seeds, cinnamon, star anise, black pepper, coriander, salt, olive oil, and brown sugar. Blend until smooth.

2 Place the cubed lamb into a medium bowl and pour the marinade through a fine-mesh sieve over it. Mix to coat, transfer to the fridge, and let marinate for at least 1 hour and up to 4 hours.

3 Snugly skewer 5 pieces of the marinated lamb onto each skewer, for a total of 8 skewers. Place the skewers onto a plate and spoon the extra marinade over each skewer to coat evenly. Set aside or hold in the fridge for up to 4 hours, until ready to grill.

4 Preheat a grill to high heat.[3]

5 Grill the skewers on all 4 sides, 1 to 2 minutes per side. Transfer to a serving dish.

6 **Toss the watercress salad:** In a small bowl, toss together the watercress, lemon juice, olive oil, sesame seeds, and salt.

7 Top the skewers with dressed watercress, finish with the lemon wedges, and serve.

1
Carob molasses is a sweet and somewhat chocolaty syrup made from the carob fruit. You can probably find it at any nice grocery store but definitely at any Middle Eastern market. When all else fails, consult the internet!

2
If some pieces are bigger or smaller, all good. No one need be concerned with perfection.

3
You may want to rub the grates with a lightly oiled cloth to help prevent the skewers from sticking.

Lamb Meatballs
with Soggy Steak Fries

There are plenty of simple meatball recipes out there, and this is one of them. But we had to go the distance and add one key component: a broth. Why? Because we like to eat our meatballs with a spoon, we love soggy steak fries, and we are big fans of juicy things in general. We recognize it's a steeper hill to climb, but once you reach the top of meatball mountain, we think you'll see why we took you on the path less traveled.

Get Ahead

The broth and meatballs can be made ahead and reheated, leaving just the last-minute task of roasting some potatoes at mealtime.

Broth

3 cups chicken stock
¼ lemon
1 bay leaf
1 sprig oregano
6 garlic cloves, smashed
½ yellow onion, root intact
1 teaspoon kosher salt

Steak Fries

2 pounds Yukon Gold potatoes, cut into
      8 to 10 wedges per potato
⅓ cup olive oil
2 teaspoons kosher salt
1 garlic clove, grated on a Microplane

Meatballs

½ yellow onion, roughly chopped
Grated zest of ½ lemon
1 egg yolk
3 tablespoons whole milk
2 garlic cloves
2 teaspoons oregano, from about 6 sprigs
1 teaspoon kosher salt
¼ teaspoon freshly ground black pepper
¼ teaspoon Aleppo
¼ cup instant mashed potatoes
1 pound ground lamb
⅔ cup neutral oil, such as canola or sunflower

For Serving

½ cup parsley leaves, roughly chopped
1 lemon, cut into wedges

1

When rolling the meatballs, keep a little bowl of water handy. When your hands start to feel sticky, dab your hands with a splash of water and the meatballs will roll more smoothly.

1 **Make the broth:** In a medium pot, combine the chicken stock, lemon, bay leaf, oregano, garlic, onion, and salt. Bring to a boil over medium-high heat, then reduce the heat to medium-low and simmer for 15 minutes. Remove from the heat and let steep for at least 30 minutes. Using a slotted spoon, remove and discard the aromatics. Set the pot of broth aside.

2 **Make the steak fries:** Preheat the oven to 400°F.

3 On a baking sheet, toss the potato wedges with the olive oil and salt. Transfer to the oven and bake until golden brown, about 40 minutes, flipping halfway through.

4 Remove from the oven and add the grated garlic to the potatoes. Using a metal spatula, pry up any stuck wedges and toss to distribute the garlic.

5 **Meanwhile, make the meatballs:** In a blender, combine the onion, lemon zest, egg yolk, milk, garlic, oregano, salt, pepper, and Aleppo. Blend until there are no large pieces of onion left, about 30 seconds. Transfer to a medium bowl, add the instant potatoes, and stir to combine. Add the ground lamb and, using your hands, mix together thoroughly. Scoop out a generous tablespoon of the mixture and roll it lightly between the palms of your hands to form a meatball.[1] Place on a plate and make the rest of the meatballs—you should end up with about 24.

6 Line a large plate with paper towels. In a large cast-iron skillet, heat the oil over medium-high heat. Working in batches, fry the meatballs, turning to brown all sides, about 15 minutes per batch. Using a slotted spoon, remove the meatballs to the paper towels to drain.

7 When all of the meatballs are fried and drained, return the pot of broth to the stove. Drop the meatballs into the broth and bring up to a light boil over medium-high heat. Reduce the heat to low and gently simmer for 10 minutes.

8 **To serve:** Divide the steak fries among four shallow bowls. Top with even amounts of meatballs and broth, followed by parsley. Serve with a lemon wedge.

Lamb-Spice Lamb Chops

Lamb Spice—or known by its official back-of-house title, Top Secret Lamb Spice—was the reigning flavor champion of the daytime menu at Kismet. We used TSLS to flavor lamby bits that got tucked into a tuft of creamy Freekeh "Polenta" (page 186) with a bit of grilled cabbage, and loyal customers still ask after that dish wistfully. Maybe we'll reintroduce it someday if we revive our daytime menu, but in the meantime, we've done a stripped-back, dinner-ready reinvention with lamb chops, and it's bringing back all the feels. Serving the polenta alongside, while not a requirement, would be a slam dunk.

Lamb Spice

2 tablespoons ground coriander

2 teaspoons ground cumin

1 teaspoon ground caraway

¼ teaspoon freshly ground black pepper

½ teaspoon ground fennel seed

1 tablespoon kosher salt

8 to 12 lamb rib chops (about 2 pounds total)

8 tablespoons olive oil

1 garlic clove, grated on a Microplane

1 lemon, halved

1 small head cabbage, cut into 12 wedges, core intact

2 teaspoons kosher salt

1 **Make the lamb spice:** In a small bowl, combine the coriander, cumin, caraway, black pepper, fennel, and salt. Mix to combine.

2 On a plate, rub the lamb chops with 2 tablespoons of the olive oil, evenly coating all sides. Sprinkle the lamb spice evenly over the chops, coating all of the surfaces. Transfer the seasoned chops, uncovered, to the fridge for at least 1 hour (and up to 3 hours).

3 In a small bowl, combine 4 tablespoons of the olive oil and the grated garlic. Let sit for at least 30 minutes.

4 Preheat a grill to medium heat. While it's heating up, grill the lemon halves, about 10 minutes total, until deeply caramelized. Set aside.

5 Rub the cabbage wedges with the remaining 2 tablespoons olive oil and sprinkle with the salt. Grill for 5 minutes per side. Transfer the cooked cabbage to a serving dish and, using a pastry brush, brush the garlic oil[1] onto the hot cabbage.

6 Turn the grill up to high heat, allowing it to come up to temp for 5 to 10 minutes.[2]

7 Grill the chops, 2 to 4 minutes per side, to medium-rare/medium.[3]

8 Transfer the chops from the grill onto the cabbage and allow to rest for 3 to 5 minutes. Serve with the grilled lemon.

[1] When you brush on the oil, try to avoid most of the garlic solids. You want the flavor of the garlic without so much intensity.

[2] Your grill should be really cranking. The hot-hot heat will help you get good color on the chops, without overcooking them.

[3] That said, it can be hard *not* to overcook a lamb chop, especially the teeny-tiny ones. Luckily, they're delicious regardless.

Breaded + Braised Pork Chops

Normally, we wouldn't braise a quick-cooking cut like a chop, but this recipe has history. The technique comes from my father's mother, Grandma Bea, who passed away before I was born. Though I was named after her (Beatrice is my middle name, and Sara was hers), I've known her only through stories and the few recipes of hers that have lived on. Along with her stellar apple cake, a forever family favorite, is this unique breaded braise: the ultimate cold-weather comfort food. There's something deeply satisfying in how the crisp coating becomes a sponge, softening and soaking up all of the tasty juice. Texturally, think tempura in soba, croissants in coffee, cookies in milk!

Grandma Bea made it with veal chops, but (for shame) we've opted for pork instead. It's much easier to source an ethical cut of pork than veal, and also (sorry, Grandma) the richness of pork fat makes this version especially tasty. But by all means, veal it up if you want to go full grandma. It also works with chicken legs, and—fun fact—that variation was the first dish I ever contributed to a restaurant menu (shout-out to Diner in Williamsburg, circa 2009). I can't recall what I served it with then, but a few buttered potatoes and a watercress salad would round out any version nicely. —Sara Kramer

4 boneless pork loin chops,[1] ¾ inch thick
    (about 8 ounces each)

1 tablespoon plus 2 teaspoons kosher salt

½ cup all-purpose flour

2 large eggs, beaten

3 cups bread crumbs or lightly crushed panko

1 cup neutral oil, such as canola or sunflower

2 cups thinly sliced yellow onion (about
    1 onion)

4 garlic cloves, chopped

¼ teaspoon freshly ground black pepper

3 cups sauerkraut

½ cup sauerkraut juice

½ cup white wine

2 cups chicken stock

1 tablespoon Dijon mustard

1 bay leaf

1. Lay the pork chops on a plate and season them evenly on both sides with 1 tablespoon of the salt.

2. Set up a dredging station in three wide shallow dishes, placing the flour in one, the beaten eggs in the second, and the bread crumbs in the third. Dip each chop into the flour first, shaking off the excess, then coat with the egg, draining off any excess before transferring to the bread crumbs, pressing the chops lightly into the crumbs to coat.

3. Preheat the oven to 300°F.

4. In a large Dutch oven, heat the neutral oil over medium-high heat until shimmering, about 5 minutes. Working in batches, fry the pork chops for 4 minutes per side, until fully golden brown. Once all of the chops are fried, carefully discard (or save to reuse) all but 2 tablespoons of the oil.

5. Reduce the heat to medium, add the onion, garlic, black pepper, and remaining 2 teaspoons salt, and sauté, stirring occasionally, until softened, 5 to 7 minutes.

6. Stir in the sauerkraut, sauerkraut juice, wine, chicken stock, mustard, and bay leaf. Nestle the pork chops, side by side, into the sauerkraut, pressing down to make sure the chops are covered in liquid. Cover with a lid or foil and transfer to the oven.

7. Bake for 1½ hours. Uncover and bake until tender, 20 to 30 minutes longer. Let sit at room temp for 15 minutes before serving.

1
You can definitely make this with a more classic braise cut, like pork shoulder—just be sure it's cut into chops.

Not-Sweet Stuffed Cabbage

We're big on cabbage, and we love the *idea* of stuffing cabbage because, c'mon, a chubby little leaf parcel is just charming. We both grew up with sweet, tomato-based stuffed cabbage, and with all due respect to tradition, we've opted to develop an ultrasavory version instead. Packed with earthy buckwheat and sharp sauerkraut, this is a dish we will happily eat any night of the week.

4 cups chicken stock

½ teaspoon plus 1 teaspoon kosher salt

⅓ cup short-grain white rice

¼ cup buckwheat groats

1 tablespoon olive oil

1½ cups diced yellow onion
    (about 1 medium onion)

4 garlic cloves, chopped

½ pound ground beef (20% fat)

¾ cup sauerkraut

½ cup sauerkraut juice

½ cup white wine

¼ cup soy sauce

3 tablespoons distilled white vinegar

½ teaspoon freshly ground black pepper

1 head cabbage

2 tablespoons unsalted butter, cubed

2 cups full-fat sour cream

¼ cup dill leaves

1   In a medium pot, combine the chicken stock and ½ teaspoon of the salt and bring to a boil over medium-high heat. Add the rice and buckwheat groats, reduce the temperature to medium-low, and simmer for 15 minutes. Pour the cooked grains into a fine-mesh sieve set over a bowl. Set both the cooking liquid and the grains aside.

2   Meanwhile, in a skillet, heat the olive oil over medium-low heat. Add the onion, garlic, and remaining 1 teaspoon salt and cook, stirring occasionally, until the onion is lightly caramelized, about 15 minutes.

3   Add the ground beef to the skillet, stirring constantly with a whisk to break the meat up into pebbly bits, and cook for 10 minutes. Add the sauerkraut, sauerkraut juice, white wine, soy sauce, vinegar, and black pepper. Increase the heat to medium and reduce the liquid until it has mostly evaporated. Mix in the cooked rice and buckwheat, remove from the heat, and let cool to room temp.

4   While the filling cools, bring 12 cups of water to a simmer in a large pot over medium heat. Remove the core of the cabbage using a paring knife, cutting into the cabbage in a conical shape. Place the whole head of cabbage in the simmering water, cored-side down. (The cabbage will only be partially covered in water.) After about a minute or two, as the leaves start to soften, use metal tongs to pull them away from the head. Dip them in the hot water a little longer to soften them, before pulling them out and placing them in a colander set over a bowl.[1] Drain the excess water from them. Choose 12 nice large leaves for the rolls, along with extras for lining the baking dish, and let cool.

5   Preheat the oven to 325°F.

1
The process of pulling the leaves away from the head of cabbage may seem a little tedious, and it does require your full attention. But it's actually pretty meditative once you get into it, and it doesn't take too long.

6   When the leaves are cool enough to handle, flatten the larger leaves on a cutting board and, using a paring knife, shave off some of the thick, stemmy vein at the center to help make the whole leaf evenly flat and easier to roll. Line the bottom and edges of a 9 × 11-inch baking dish or a medium Dutch oven with the extra leaves not reserved for rolling.

7   Flatten a rolling leaf on a surface and place a heaping ¼ cup of filling in the center. First fold the sides in over the filling, then roll the bottom up snugly around the filling toward the top. Repeat with all 12 leaves, fitting the rolls snugly into the leaf-lined dish. Cover them in the reserved grain-cooking liquid and dot with the butter.

8   Bake until the rolls are nicely browned on top, with a little liquid left in the pan, about 2 hours. They should be soft enough to cut through easily.

9   Remove from the oven and let cool for 20 minutes. Serve topped with a generous dollop of sour cream and dill.

Beefy Lentil Stew

This heavy-on-the-comfort, lightly spiced stew combines the Turkish flavors of sumac and dried mint with the creamy finish of an Indian dal makhani. It's the kind of simple but satisfying stew that you want to curl up with for a cozy night in. Basmati rice makes the perfect partner here, and any bread you have on hand would make a fine accompaniment as well. This recipe calls for butter and cream, but we might even suggest tripling down on the dairy by garnishing your bowl with a dollop of yogurt.

1 pound beef stew meat,
    cut into 1-inch cubes
2 teaspoons plus 1 tablespoon kosher salt
2 tablespoons neutral oil, such as
    canola or sunflower
4 tablespoons unsalted butter
2 cups diced white onion (about 1 onion)
8 garlic cloves, chopped
1 bunch cilantro, stems minced and leaves
    reserved to finish
1 bay leaf
1 tablespoon Aleppo
1 tablespoon dried mint
1 tablespoon sumac
1½ teaspoons ground coriander
¼ cup tomato paste
1 cup canned crushed tomatoes
4 cups beef or chicken stock[1]
⅔ cup French green or black lentils
¾ cup heavy cream

1. Season the meat with 2 teaspoons of the salt.

2. In a Dutch oven, heat the oil over medium-high heat. Working in two batches, brown the meat on all sides, about 10 minutes total. Set the browned meat aside.

3. Reduce the heat to medium-low. Add the butter, onion, garlic, cilantro stems, bay leaf, Aleppo, dried mint, sumac, coriander, and the remaining 1 tablespoon salt. Sauté for 15 minutes, stirring often. Stir in the tomato paste to combine.

4. Return the beef to the pot. Add the crushed tomatoes and stock. Cover and simmer over low heat until the beef is tender, about 1½ hours.

5. When the beef has about 30 minutes to go, in a saucepot, combine the lentils and 3 cups water and bring up to a boil. Reduce the heat to low and simmer until tender, 30 to 45 minutes.[2]

6. Once the beef is tender, pour the lentils (along with any cooking liquid) into the beef, stir together, and simmer for 15 minutes.

7. Stir in the cream, top with cilantro leaves, and serve.

1
If you're using store-bought stock, look for something that's just bones (i.e., bone broth but without the salt). Most packaged stocks also contain vegetables, which can muddy up the flavor. You could also use water instead of stock.

2
Err on the side of overcooked for the lentils. It's a stew, after all, so letting them break down a bit is preferable.

Weeknight Steak with Grapes + Grilled Peppers

Sometimes even a weeknight calls for some steaky celebration, and a grilled pepper salad makes the ideal, just-casual-enough side. If you want to be even more midweek about it, you could easily keep the peppers raw, but we prefer the just-cooked texture of a quick kiss on the grill. Tossed with the grapes, thyme, and Urfa pepper, they're a light yet satisfying partner to your protein.

Steak

2 tablespoons olive oil

2 garlic cloves, grated on a Microplane

2 teaspoons kosher salt

1 teaspoon Urfa pepper

2 steaks (10 ounces each), such as strip or hanger

Peppers + Grapes

2 bell peppers, any color

1 teaspoon plus ¼ cup olive oil

2½ teaspoons kosher salt

2 cups green grapes, halved

½ yellow onion, thinly sliced

3 tablespoons lemon juice (about 1½ lemons)

½ teaspoon Urfa pepper

½ teaspoon thyme leaves

1 **Marinate the steaks:** In a wide dish, combine the olive oil, grated garlic, salt, and Urfa pepper. Add the steaks and rub the marinade into them, coating evenly. Transfer the dish to the fridge and let it sit for at least 1 hour and up to 4 hours. Pull the steak from the fridge to come to room temp for 30 minutes before grilling.

2 Preheat a grill to high heat.

3 **Grill the peppers:** In a small bowl, coat the bell peppers with 1 teaspoon of the olive oil. Sprinkle ½ teaspoon of the salt evenly over them. Grill the peppers, turning occasionally, to lightly char all sides, 6 to 8 minutes.

4 When the peppers are cool enough to handle, cut them in half and discard the stems and seeds. Cut into bite-size pieces and place in a medium bowl.

5 Grill the steaks over high heat, until nicely charred and medium-rare to medium, 4 to 5 minutes per side. Transfer the steaks to a serving plate and let them rest for 5 to 10 minutes.

6 Add the grapes to the bowl of peppers, along with the onion, lemon juice, Urfa pepper, thyme, and the remaining ¼ cup olive oil. Add the remaining 2 teaspoons salt and toss.

7 Slice the steaks[1] and serve topped with the pepper-grape salad.

1
If you'd like to finish the steaks with a little flaky sea salt, a sliced steak always welcomes a bit.

The Rabbit

In 2012, when I was approached to be the chef of Glasserie, the very first dish I created for the menu was this rabbit. The legs gently confited in duck fat, the loins spiced and skewered, and all of the extra bits stewed gently with chickpeas and a turmeric-heavy spice blend called hawaij, this dish is a celebration. Giving rabbit a platform on which to shine made it a hit from day one—it made the headline of Glasserie's *New York Times* write-up, and Sarah and I liked it enough to bring it across the country to Kismet.

Rabbit, you might be thinking, is a niche choice. For sure, and that's the point. I had seen plenty of whole chickens and fish on restaurant menus, large-format steaks and roasts, but never a big-deal rabbit. It's somewhat understandable because, as we all know, bunnies are very cute and therefore a tough sell. But they're also an environmentally friendly, sustainable, healthy, and delicious protein choice. If we all decided to eat them more often, they would also be more readily available and affordable. Alas, they're still something of a luxury, so we encourage you to cook this for a special occasion—or make an occasion out of cooking a rabbit!

While there are several steps involved here, breaking down the bunny is probably the hardest part. If you're not up for the task, ask a butcher to cut it for you into legs, loins, and trim (the meat from the bellies and other bits), and have them save you the bones. Serve your small feast with Flaky Bread (page 224), a generous scoop of labneh, and we always encourage pickles. —Sara Kramer

See photo on page 218.

Get Ahead

The hawaij blend keeps for weeks in an airtight container.

The confit and stew can be cooked up to 3 days ahead and reheated.

Hawaij Spice Blend
2 teaspoons ground turmeric
1 teaspoon ground caraway
1 teaspoon ground cardamom
1 teaspoon ground coriander
1 teaspoon ground cumin
1 teaspoon freshly ground black pepper

1 whole rabbit (3 to 4 pounds), broken down
 into 4 legs, 2 loins, and trim

Confit Rabbit Legs
2 teaspoons kosher salt
2 cups duck fat
2 bay leaves
½ lemon
1 teaspoon coriander seeds
2 teaspoons sesame seeds
1 teaspoon nigella seeds

1. **Make the hawaij spice blend:** In a small bowl, combine the turmeric, caraway, cardamom, coriander, cumin, and black pepper. Mix thoroughly and set aside.

2. Set the 4 rabbit legs (front and back legs) aside for the confit. Cut the trim into 1- to 2-inch pieces and set aside for the stew. Cut the loins into 1-inch cubes for 12 to 16 pieces total and set aside for the skewers.

3. Preheat the oven to 275°F.

4. **Confit the rabbit legs:** In a small ovenproof pan, snugly lay the rabbit legs flat and sprinkle with the salt, distributing evenly. Let sit for 15 to 20 minutes.

5. In a small pot, melt the duck fat and pour it over the rabbit legs. Add the bay leaves and lemon, cover tightly with foil, and cook for 2 hours. Uncover and cook until fork-tender, another 30 minutes.

6. Meanwhile, in a small pot, toast the coriander seeds for 2 minutes, swirling over medium heat. Transfer to a mortar and pestle to cool. Next, add the sesame seeds to the pan and toast for 2 minutes, swirling, until lightly golden. Transfer to a small bowl. Lightly crush the coriander seeds to crack them open, then mix together with the toasted sesame and nigella seeds. Set aside.

Stew

2 tablespoons olive oil

2 cups diced yellow onions (about 1½ onions)

2 teaspoons kosher salt

1 teaspoon tomato paste

1 cup diced tomato (about 1 large tomato)

2 cups chicken stock[1]

1 (15-ounce) can chickpeas, drained

Skewers

1 summer squash or zucchini, cut into
    ½-inch rounds or half-moons

2 tablespoons olive oil

1½ teaspoons kosher salt

1 teaspoon sweet paprika

1 teaspoon hot paprika

For Serving

2 tablespoons olive oil

1 head butter lettuce, leaves separated

1 cup cilantro leaves

½ cup mint leaves

2 tablespoons lemon juice (about 1 lemon)

½ teaspoon kosher salt

1 lemon, halved, for squeezing

7 **Make the stew:** In a medium pot, combine the olive oil, onions, and salt. Cook over medium-low heat, stirring frequently, for 15 minutes.

8 Add 2 tablespoons of the hawaij spice blend to the pot of onions and cook for 4 more minutes. Stir in the tomato paste to dissolve it, then stir in the fresh tomato, reserved rabbit trim, and chicken stock. Bring to a boil over medium-high heat, then reduce the heat to medium-low and simmer until the meat is tender and the stew is pleasantly rich and concentrated in flavor, about 1½ hours. Stir in the chickpeas and simmer for 10 more minutes.

9 **Assemble the skewers:** In a medium bowl, combine the reserved cubes of rabbit loin and the summer squash pieces. Add the olive oil, salt, 1 teaspoon of the hawaij spice blend, the sweet paprika, and hot paprika and toss to coat. Let sit for 30 minutes to soften.

10 Skewer the pieces onto 4 skewers, alternating the rabbit and squash pieces for a total of 3 or 4 of each per skewer. Let marinate in the fridge for 30 minutes or up to 4 hours.

11 **To serve:** In a cast-iron skillet, heat 1 tablespoon of the olive oil over medium-high heat for 2 to 3 minutes until shimmering. Cook each skewer until just cooked through, 1½ minutes per side.

12 In a salad bowl, combine the lettuce, cilantro, and mint. Dress with the lemon juice, salt, and the remaining 1 tablespoon of the olive oil and toss to coat.

13 Arrange the skewers on a platter. Set the confit legs next to the skewers and top the legs with the reserved seed mixture. Plate the dressed salad next to the rabbit pieces. Transfer the stew to a serving bowl and serve all together with the halved lemon.

[1]
You can fortify your chicken stock with the rabbit bones if you like. Roast the bones in a 400°F oven until golden brown. Place them into a medium saucepan and cover with the stock and 2 cups water. Simmer for 1 to 1½ hours; you want to end up with 2 cups total stock. Strain through a fine-mesh sieve.

Rice, Bread + Friends

The most popular things on our menus consistently fall under one category: Rice, Bread + Friends. In this chapter, you'll find those greatest hits—including a single, but iconic, rice dish—plus more of our favorite flaky and fried favorites, from handheld pies to latkes. Many of these recipes are fun little projects where much of the work can be done ahead and kept frozen, ready to bake (or grill or fry) when the moment calls.

Persian-Style Crispy Rice

This rice—a version of tahchin, the classic saffron-scented, tahdig-topped Persian rice—holds the title for Kismet's most popular dish. (It's worth noting that though it's often confused, the tahdig is just the coveted crunchy part, while the whole dish is known as tahchin.) We started developing this version in 2013 when we worked together at Glasserie, but we didn't really find our footing with it until we were rounding the corner to opening day at Kismet, years later. We needed a version that could be made to order and portioned individually, with an eye-catching, perfectly bronzed dome. As for the oozy egg yolk addition, well, we never want to miss out on the opportunity to put on a little show.

This is our interpretation, and not a strictly traditional representation, of Persian rice. It is a celebration of our love of crispy (or scorched) rice across many cuisines, Persian rice being the most direct reference. There are a number of wonderful, more traditional tahchin/tahdig recipes out there; we particularly want to steer you in Najmieh Batmanglij's direction. Her cookbooks (especially *Food of Life* and *New Food of Life*) are tomes of Persian cooking and up there with the greatest cookbooks of all time.

One last important detail for success with this version is the pan. Invest in an 8-inch nonstick pan that has a lid with a hole to let the steam escape, which is crucial for achieving the most shatteringly crisp crust, and that's what we're looking for.

1¾ cups basmati rice

3 tablespoons plus ¼ teaspoon kosher salt

1 bay leaf

2 teaspoons annatto seeds, tied in cheesecloth[1]

½ cup pumpkin seeds

1 teaspoon olive oil

½ cup dried currants

2 tablespoons red wine vinegar

2 teaspoons sugar

Crust Mixture

1 tablespoon Greek yogurt

4 tablespoons butter, at room temperature

2 teaspoons rice flour

To Finish

3 egg yolks

1 Fill a medium bowl with water. Add the rice and, using your hand, swirl to release the starch. Pour through a fine-mesh sieve and rinse thoroughly with water.

2 In a large pot, combine 8 cups water, 3 tablespoons of the salt, the bay leaf, and annatto seeds and bring to a boil over high heat. Reduce the heat to medium, add the rice, and stir to keep it from sticking to the bottom. Cook for 7 minutes, stirring occasionally. Drain the parcooked rice in a fine-mesh sieve and spread it out onto a baking sheet. Cool in the freezer for 15 to 20 minutes (or in the fridge for 45 minutes).

3 Preheat the oven to 300°F.

4 While the rice is cooling, on a baking sheet, toss together the pumpkin seeds, olive oil, and remaining ¼ teaspoon salt. Toast in the oven for 30 minutes, until lightly fragrant.

5 At the same time, in a small pot, combine the currants, vinegar, and sugar and cook over medium heat, stirring until syrupy, 2 to 3 minutes. Turn off the heat and let sit, covered, to fully absorb.

6 **Make the crust mixture:** In a small bowl, combine the Greek yogurt, 2 tablespoons of the softened butter, rice flour, and 2 teaspoons

---

1

You can use a tea ball instead of cheesecloth, if you have one. Either way, it needs to be sealed well, to be sure that the annatto doesn't escape its pouch.

2

If your lid is firmly pressed into the rice, you'll run the risk of having the crispy bits stick to the edges and break your perfect crust.

water and stir thoroughly into a sticky paste. Add 1¼ cups cooked rice to the yogurt mixture and mix to coat evenly.

7   Pour the rice crust mixture onto the bottom of an 8-inch nonstick pan. Using the back of a spoon, pull it toward the edges of the pan. Scrape the rice mixture up the sides, to flatten against the entire perimeter, before patting down the center. (It helps to have a little bowl of hot water handy—a quick dip helps to keep the rice from sticking to your spoon.)

8   Gently spread half of the remaining rice on top of the formed crust. Scatter half of both the pumpkin seeds and currants over that layer (set the remaining pumpkin seeds and currants aside). Top with the remaining rice. Place the pan over medium heat, gently place the pan's lid over the rice,[2] and cook for 5 minutes.

9   In a small pan, melt the remaining two tablespoons of butter. After the rice has been cooking for 5 minutes, remove the lid and spoon the melted butter around the perimeter of the pan. Gently place the lid back onto the rice, reduce the heat to medium-low, and cook for 25 minutes longer, rotating the pan occasionally for even browning.

10 **To finish:** Uncover and use a spoon to make a divot in the center of the rice. Gently drop the yolks into the hole and ever-so-gently cover them up with rice. Turn off the heat, invert a serving plate over the pan, and flip the rice out onto it.

11 Top with the remaining currants and pumpkin seeds and serve immediately.

Flaky Bread (Malawach)

I grew up eating malawach—a rich, flaky flatbread of Yemeni origin—for weekend breakfast. It's no exaggeration to say it was *the* treat I loved and looked forward to most. My mom has, in recent years, claimed that she would make malawach from scratch when I was young, but all I remember is the store-bought stuff we'd trek out to deep Brooklyn to get. We'd buy stacks of it and keep them stashed in the freezer. As a kid, pulling a piece out and frying it up myself gave me a sense of feeling quite competent in the kitchen.

We'd eat malawach slathered generously with labneh and Red Zhoug (page 92), accompanied by a fresh grated tomato sauce seasoned with just salt and olive oil. While I can't say there's a better way to go than that, you might also want a piece or two alongside any of the marinated feta options (see pages 44 to 51) or to swoosh through the spices in the Moroccan-Spiced Carrots (page 142). Malawach pairs excellently with almost anything, especially if there's some dairy and spice in the mix.

While you're probably unlikely to find malawach in a freezer section near you, I encourage you to experience this pretty perfect food by making it yourself. The process here is 100 percent a labor of love, but the reward is rich. Stash a bag of malawach in your freezer, and you've got a buttery gold mine, ready to provide a sense of accomplishment every time you pop one in a pan. —Sara Kramer

Get Ahead

Here, we're freezing the fully prepared dough to have it at the ready whenever you need a perfect piece of flaky, buttery bread in 15 minutes flat. These keep in the freezer for 3 months.

---

3 cups all-purpose flour

1¾ cups pastry flour[1]

2 tablespoons kosher salt

1 tablespoon plus 1 teaspoon sugar

½ teaspoon baking powder

4 sticks (16 ounces) unsalted butter,[2] at room temperature

1 In a stand mixer fitted with the dough hook, whisk together the all-purpose flour, pastry flour, salt, sugar, and baking powder. With the mixer on low speed, slowly pour 1¾ cups cold water into the dry ingredients, bringing the dough together. Increase the speed to medium and knead until the dough is homogeneous and smooth, about 5 minutes.

2 While the dough is kneading, lightly butter (about 1 teaspoon) a medium bowl. Place the finished dough in this bowl and cover with plastic wrap. Let rest at room temperature for 1½ hours.

3 After resting, flip the dough out onto a lightly buttered surface and cut into 12 equal portions. Shape each one into a ball and coat with a sheen of softened butter (no need to measure, just a light layer so the dough doesn't dry out). Place each one onto a greased baking sheet, cover tightly with plastic, and let rest for 1 hour.

1
Using pastry flour yields a slightly more tender result, but if you don't have it on hand, you can replace it with the same amount of all-purpose.

2
You may end up with a little leftover butter at the end, but we wanted to make sure you had plenty for all of the purposes — from greasing the various surfaces to making the dough.

3
Your dough may tear in an effort to get it nice and thin — that's okay! Do your best to stretch the dough carefully, but ultimately, when you roll it up, you won't notice the tears.

4   Using your hands, grease a baking sheet and a clean work surface with a tablespoon of butter each. Working with one portion at a time, using your buttery palms, spread the dough out very thinly onto the work surface into a rough rectangle. Spread about 1 teaspoon of butter on the surface of the dough as you work to help the dough spread more easily, ignoring tears in the dough.[3] Once fully stretched, it should measure about 12 × 18 inches, with the short side facing you. Spread about 1 tablespoon of butter thinly and evenly over the stretched dough.

5   Starting from the bottom (the 12-inch side) and working toward the top, fold the dough in 2- to 3-inch strips over itself (should be 5 to 6 folds), ending in one long strip, then roll it over itself into a tight snail and place it onto the greased baking sheet. You want the smooth side up (not the swirl side). Repeat with the other pieces. Wrap the finished tray and refrigerate overnight or up to 24 hours.

6   After chilling, on a clean surface, roll each dough portion into a 4-inch by 5-inch rectangle, ⅛ to ¼ inch thick. (Use a bench scraper, if you have one, to move the dough as you work to avoid too much sticking.) As you finish each piece, place it between sheets of parchment and transfer to the freezer to fully freeze for 6 hours or up to 24.

7   Once frozen, remove the dough pieces from the parchment and store together in a large resealable plastic bag in the freezer.

8   When ready to cook, heat a cast-iron skillet or griddle over medium heat. Once hot, add the frozen piece of dough and cook for about 15 minutes, flipping several times to get even color on both sides.

Grilled Flatbread

We've made many flatbreads over the years, but we like the sturdiness of this recipe, which comes from the extra strength of bread flour. These are not only great for dipping and sopping but also for wrapping into sandwiches. This recipe was, in fact, the one we used for the sandwiches at our falafel spot in Grand Central Market. Even after the years of stacks upon stacks of dough balls, we're always happy to have an opportunity to roll up a batch.

Like most flatbreads, these are best eaten right off the grill. But if you're saving them for later, wrap a stack of them tightly in plastic while they're still warm—steaming them this way keeps them pliable and tender. You can refresh them by quickly throwing them back on the grill. If you want an even more eye-catching centerpiece, brush them with olive oil and dust with za'atar or any spice/seed blend you have on hand.

Get Ahead

You can make the dough either earlier in the day or a day ahead and refrigerate it after portioning. Pull it from the fridge 30 to 60 minutes (the hotter the ambient temperature, the faster it proofs) before you're ready to roll.

2 teaspoons active dry yeast

1½ teaspoons sugar

2 cups bread flour,[1] plus more for dusting

½ cup whole wheat flour

1 teaspoon kosher salt

3 tablespoons olive oil, plus more for the proofing bowl

1 Mix the yeast and sugar into 1 cup warm water and let sit until foamy, about 5 minutes.

2 In a large bowl, whisk together the bread flour, whole wheat flour, and salt.

3 Add the olive oil to the water/yeast mixture and pour into the flour mixture. Knead by hand on a lightly floured surface (or on low speed in a stand mixer fitted with the dough hook) until the dough springs back when poked, about 15 minutes.

4 Transfer the dough to a lightly oiled large bowl and cover tightly with plastic wrap. Let rise at room temp until doubled in size, 1 to 1½ hours (depending on the ambient temp).

5 Portion the dough into 6 equal pieces and transfer to a lightly floured baking sheet. Loosely wrap with plastic (keeping it airtight but leaving enough room to grow) and proof until doubled, 30 to 45 minutes.

6 Preheat a grill to high heat.

7 On a surface generously dusted with flour, roll the flatbread out to a round about ¼ inch thick.[2] Grill for 45 to 60 seconds per side, flipping once puffed and then as needed to avoid burning. Serve immediately.

1
If all you have is all-purpose flour, you can use it in place of bread flour. The end result will be a little more tender.

2
Keep your dough disk moving while you roll. You want to avoid letting it stick to the counter.

Three-Cheese Borekas

There's not a recipe in the world that tastes more like home to me than this one. These borekas (or borekitas, as my mother likes to call them) are a nonpareil, pillow-shaped, two-bite comfort food. I grew up making them with my safta (Hebrew for grandmother) whenever she came to visit from Panama, and to this day, my mother makes big batches, freezes them, and has toaster oven–ready snacks on hand for any hungry visitor. They're of Sephardic origin, shaped like mini empanadas, and though they share an etymology, they're quite different from Turkish borek, which are more typically made with doughs similar to phyllo, yufka, or puff pastry. This is a yeasted, enriched dough: tender and buttery, light and also rich, quite specific and special. I could easily eat half a dozen of these as an afternoon snack with a cup of sweetened anise tea and feel transported to simpler times.

Folding the fluffy cheese into each little pocket and crimping the edges is a meditation for me. The movement is so deeply familiar that I barely need to look down, but it might take anyone new to the task a little practice at first. The dough is pretty forgiving, so give it a few goes and don't give up—wonky edges won't make them any less tasty. —Sara Kramer

⅓ cup whole milk

Pinch of sugar

2 teaspoons active dry yeast

2½ cups all-purpose flour, plus more for rolling out the dough

1 tablespoon plus ⅛ teaspoon kosher salt

1 stick (4 ounces) unsalted butter, cut into pieces

⅓ cup heavy cream

½ cup ricotta cheese

¼ cup crumbled feta cheese

¼ cup grated Parmesan cheese

⅛ teaspoon freshly ground black pepper

1 large egg

3 tablespoons sesame seeds

1　In a small saucepan, lightly heat the milk and sugar until it feels warm to the touch but not hot. Remove from the heat and stir in the yeast. Let it bloom until foamy, about 5 minutes.

2　Meanwhile, in a medium bowl, whisk together the flour and 1 tablespoon of the salt. Using a pastry cutter, work the butter into the flour mixture until incorporated. The texture should be sandy with the butter broken down into very small pieces. (Alternatively, you can pulse in a food processor.)

3　Pour the yeast mixture into the flour bowl, along with the cream. Stir using a wooden spoon, then bring the dough together with your hands. Knead until all of the ingredients are incorporated evenly, no more than a minute or two. Return the dough to the bowl, cover in plastic wrap, and let rise for 2 hours.[1]

4　While the dough is rising, in a medium bowl, combine the ricotta, feta, Parmesan, pepper, and remaining ⅛ teaspoon salt. Mix until fully incorporated.

5　In a small bowl, whisk the egg. Add half of it to the cheese mixture, mix to combine, and cover and place in the fridge to chill. Cover the remaining egg and refrigerate to use later as an egg wash.

1　Your dough may not double in size because of all of the butter and cream, but it should puff at least some amount.

2　A basic tenet for anyone who's rolled out dough: You want to be very careful not to let your dough stick to the counter. Flipping the dough once or twice while rolling is a good idea.

3　Press around the whole edge firmly, then working your way from one side to the other, pinch and fold toward the far edge. If this feels too tricky, using a fork to crimp the edges gets the job done.

6 Once the dough has risen, divide it in half. Press each half into a disk, wrap in plastic wrap, and refrigerate for at least 1 hour (and up to 24 hours).

7 When ready to use, remove one of the dough disks from the fridge and let come to room temp for 30 to 45 minutes. Unwrap and place on a lightly floured surface. Roll out the dough to a round between ⅛ and ¼ inch thick, being careful to lift and move the dough to keep it from sticking as you roll.[2]

8 Using a 3-inch pastry cutter or an upside-down glass, cut rounds out of the dough, punching them out as close together as possible. Lift the scraps and press them together into a new disk to roll out and cut more rounds. (Refrigerate the scraps disk for 10 to 15 minutes to make it easier to handle, if need be.)

9 Spoon 1 teaspoon of cheese filling onto each pastry round. Fold the round over into a half-moon and press firmly to stick the dough seam together. Using your fingers, crimp the edges into a spiral pattern.[3] Place the pastries on a parchment-lined baking sheet and refrigerate for at least 30 minutes. Repeat steps 7 through 9 with the second disk of dough.

10 Preheat the oven to 400°F.

11 Using a pastry brush, brush each pastry with the reserved beaten egg. Top each one with a generous scatter of sesame seeds.

12 Bake until golden, 12 to 14 minutes.

Spicy Carrot Borek

Borek can refer to any number of flaky, filled pastries across the Middle East, Balkans, and North Africa. They're typically filled with some combination of meat, cheese, potatoes, or greens, but the variations are endless. At first, we toyed with a meat version because we were excited to title the recipe Beefy Borek, but after several iterations, we found we much preferred this version. Brighter, lighter, and much truer to our veg-loving ways, this borek has nothing beefy about it and, we have to say, we don't miss the meat one bit. It's been swapped out in favor of sweet-spicy carrots with green olives and smoked trout. Make a meal of it with a dollop of labneh and a bright, herby salad.

Get Ahead

Once fully assembled, you can freeze the tray of borek for a later date. Cover it tightly in plastic wrap, pop it in the freezer, and, when you're ready to bake, it can go in the oven straight from frozen—just add 10 to 15 extra minutes of baking time.

Filling

1½ pounds carrots, shredded
2 teaspoons kosher salt
3 tablespoons olive oil
1 cup diced shallots (2 or 3 shallots)
4 garlic cloves, grated on a Microplane
1 tablespoon ground caraway
1 tablespoon ground coriander
1 tablespoon ground cumin
1 tablespoon plus 1 teaspoon chopped
    Calabrian chiles
6 ounces smoked trout or hot-smoked salmon
¾ cup chopped green olives, such
    as Castelvetrano
1 tablespoon plus 1 teaspoon sherry vinegar

Assembly

1 (16-ounce) package frozen phyllo dough,
    thawed overnight in the refrigerator
⅔ cup olive oil
1 egg
1 tablespoon Aleppo

1. **Make the filling:** In a medium bowl, toss the shredded carrots with the salt and let sit for 20 minutes. Using your hands, squeeze the juice from the carrots into a small bowl and set aside both.

2. Meanwhile, in a large sauté pan, heat the olive oil, shallots, garlic, caraway, coriander, and cumin and cook for 15 minutes. Pour the carrot juice into the pan. Cook, stirring frequently, until fully absorbed and reduced, 6 to 8 minutes.

3. Add the carrots and chiles and sauté for 10 minutes, stirring frequently. Remove from the heat and let cool.

4. Break the smoked trout into small bits (keeping an eye out for rogue bones). Add to the carrot mixture along with the olives and sherry vinegar and stir to combine.

5. Preheat the oven to 350°F.

6. **Assemble the borek:** Set the stack of phyllo sheets on a work surface and cover with a dry kitchen towel covered by a wrung-out damp one,[1] being careful not to let the wet towel touch the pastry sheets. Place the olive oil into a small bowl along with a pastry brush.

7. Pull one sheet of phyllo dough out onto a clean, dry surface and brush the entire sheet with oil. Starting at one of the shorter sides, lay out a heaping ⅓ cup filling in a line. Roll the pastry over the filling, tucking to tighten, until the entire sheet has been rolled into a cigar. Place on a 9 × 13-inch quarter-baking sheet—the 9-inch side should fit each roll perfectly. Continue to fill, roll, and line the cigars side by side in the tray, until all of the filling has been used—there should be 9 rolls in total and they should be tightly packed against one another and fill up the entire tray.

8. In a small bowl, whisk the egg. Brush the top of the pastry rolls with the egg wash and dust with the Aleppo.

9. Bake until golden, about 35 minutes.

1
Be sure to completely cover your stack of phyllo. It dries out in a flash, after which it's unsalvageable.

Lemony Chicken + Pine Nut Pies

The flavors in this zingy chicken pie filling were first featured in a lemony chicken soup, enjoyed a stint as toothpicked chicken meatballs, then settled into their final form: fancy hot pockets. They've been a staple on our menu ever since. Served alongside some tahini and a salad, they make a lovely lunch or dinner; as a handheld party parcel, they're great for a crowd.

Get Ahead

The chicken filling can be made up to 3 days in advance and kept in the fridge, or even longer if you freeze it. Thaw it in the fridge overnight the day before you make these.

The pies bake great from frozen, which means you can stash them away for a rainy day. Stick your baking sheets with unbaked pies in the freezer, and once the pies are fully frozen, transfer them to a resealable bag to store in the freezer. They will keep for up to 3 months frozen. Add about 3 minutes of baking time if baking from frozen.

Chicken Filling

¼ cup pine nuts
8 tablespoons olive oil
1 pound ground chicken, preferably
    dark meat
1 cup diced onion (about ½ onion)
1 cup diced leek (1 medium leek)
1 cup diced fennel (½ bulb fennel)
2 garlic cloves, grated on a Microplane
1 teaspoon chopped marjoram or
    ½ teaspoon dried
1½ teaspoons dried mint[1]
1 bay leaf
Pinch of ground cloves
Grated zest of ½ lemon
1 tablespoon plus 1 teaspoon kosher salt
¼ cup lemon juice (from about 2 lemons)

Assembly

1 (16-ounce) package frozen phyllo dough,
    thawed in the refrigerator overnight[2]
½ cup olive oil
1 large egg
¼ cup sesame seeds

1. Preheat the oven to 300°F.

2. **Make the chicken filling:** On a baking sheet, toast the pine nuts until golden, 12 to 15 minutes. Let them cool, then chop and set aside.

3. In a large pot, heat 2 tablespoons of the olive oil over medium heat for 1 minute. Add the ground chicken, stirring with a whisk to break it into pebbly bits. Cook until just cooked through, 5 to 10 minutes. Transfer the chicken, along with any juices, to a medium bowl and let cool.

4. In the same pot, heat the remaining 6 tablespoons olive oil over medium-low heat. Add the onion, leek, fennel, garlic, marjoram, mint, bay leaf, cloves, lemon zest, and salt. Cook the veg until soft, 15 to 20 minutes, stirring occasionally.

5. Add the lemon juice and pine nuts. Holding back the chicken with a spoon, pour any chicken juices that have accumulated out of the bowl and into the pot. Reduce, stirring, until the liquid has almost evaporated, 3 to 5 more minutes.

6. Discard the bay leaf. Add the cooked chicken and remove from the heat. Stir the mixture together to fully incorporate. It should be moist, but not liquidy. Transfer to a medium bowl and let cool to room temperature. Store covered in the fridge until assembly time.

7. **Assemble the pies:** Set the stack of phyllo sheets on a work surface and cover with a dry kitchen towel covered by a wrung-out damp one, being careful not to let the wet towel touch the pastry

---

[1]
Dried mint is preferable here as the flavor is different from fresh, but if fresh is all you have, it'll absolutely get the job done.

[2]
Phyllo is much harder to work with if it isn't fully thawed. Consider having a second thawed box on hand, as it's also just generally fickle.

[3]
The phyllo is nearly impossible to reposition once you lay one sheet over the first oiled sheet, so a little precision here is key.

sheets. Set up the olive oil in a small bowl with a pastry brush. Pull one sheet of the phyllo dough out onto a clean, dry surface, short sides on the bottom and top. Brush some of the oil onto the sheet in a thin even layer. Top with another sheet of the phyllo dough, laying it flat, smoothing out the air bubbles,[3] and lightly brush the top sheet with oil. Using a sharp knife, trim any dry or cracked edges and slice the double-layer of the phyllo, top to bottom, into 3 long strips each 3 to 3½ inches wide.

8 Scoop a heaping tablespoon of the chilled filling onto the bottom of each strip. Working at the edge closest to you, using the edge of your knife, lift the bottom-right corner of the strip and fold it up and over the scoop of filling to the left, forming a triangle. Take the bottom-left corner of the triangle and fold it directly up and away from you. Repeat the pattern, folding the triangle over itself and up, until you reach the end of the strip, trimming any extra phyllo off each end. Arrange the pies onto two baking sheets, leaving a little space between them to expand. Repeat until all of the filling is used and all of the pies are assembled.

9 Preheat the oven to 400°F.

10 In a small bowl, whisk the egg. Brush the pies with the egg wash a few at a time and sprinkle generously with the sesame seeds, repeating until all of the pies are sesame'd.

11 Bake until the pastry is golden brown, 10 to 12 minutes.

Not-Just-for-Chanukah Latkes

People seem to love to overcomplicate latkes, adding flour and egg and other nonsense to get them to stick together. One question: Why? These simple potato-and-onion pancakes are an ever-so-slight variation on my mom's no-frills version, and they're the best. Once you get the hang of them, you'll never look back.

Even if it's not a holiday, latkes, as a particularly interactive food, are a great opportunity for a hang. Invite your fried food–loving friends over and have them bring their favorite condiments! An array of add-ons is key. You want to be able to customize and give each latke its own special treatment. Some of my favorites are labneh (or sour cream or crème fraîche), applesauce, any herbs (dill, chives, and basil are great choices), anything pickled (bonus points for pickled chiles), chile crisp, hot sauce, and, of course, the queen of condiments: caviar. —Sara Kramer

2½ pounds russet potatoes, peeled
1 large yellow onion
1 tablespoon kosher salt
1½ cups neutral oil, such as canola or sunflower

1   Grate the potatoes and the onion into a large bowl on the large holes of a box grater. Using your hands, scoop up a handful of the potato/onion mixture and squeeze the liquid back into the bowl, then transfer the potato/onion mixture to a second large bowl. Repeat this step until the potato/onion mixture has all been squeezed and transferred. Let the bowl holding the liquid sit for 5 minutes to allow the starch to settle.

2   Pour off the excess liquid, reserving the potato starch that has accumulated at the bottom of the bowl. Add this starch and the salt to the potato/onion mixture[1] and use your hands to mix thoroughly.[2] Form the latkes into 2½- to 3-inch rounds.[3]

3   Line a plate with paper towels. In a heavy-bottomed or cast-iron skillet, heat ¾ cup of the neutral oil over medium heat. Working in batches of 3, use a spatula (or your hands, if you're comfortable) to set them into the hot oil, pressing down on the center once it's in the oil. Fry until deeply golden on both sides, 5 to 8 minutes per side, replenishing the oil as needed. Remove from the oil and set on the paper towels to drain.

4   Serve immediately.

[1] Reincorporating the potato starch helps the latkes stick together.

[2] At this point, you can set the potato mixture aside until you're ready to fry. Cover with a layer of plastic wrap pressed directly onto the mixture to avoid as much exposure to oxygen as possible.

[3] Size and shape are key! You're looking for the right creamy center/crunchy exterior balance. They should be ½ to ¾ inch thick. The edges should be a little shaggy—they're extra crunchy that way.

Guava Cheese Blintzes

Eggier and slightly thicker than crepes, these tender blintzes get a toasty flavor thanks to a kiss of brown butter. Filled with guava jam along with a traditional cottage cheese mixture, they're an ode to the delicious guava-cheese pastelitos found in the many Cuban bakeries across Los Angeles. If you can't find guava jam, feel free to sub in another. A warning: Straight from the oven, these puppies are hot!

Get Ahead

The batter can be made a day ahead and stored in the fridge; just give it a good stir before using. Once cooked, the blintzes are best eaten the same day.

The cheese filling can be made several days ahead; just wait to add the egg yolk to the filling until the day of.

Batter

1¼ cups all-purpose flour
1 tablespoon sugar
1½ teaspoons kosher salt
5 large eggs
1½ cups whole milk
2 tablespoons unsalted butter

Fillings

4 ounces cream cheese, at room temperature
1 egg yolk
1 teaspoon sugar
½ teaspoon kosher salt
2 cups full-fat cottage cheese
¾ cup guava jam
3 tablespoons lemon juice (about 1½ lemons)

Assembly

3 tablespoons unsalted butter
2 tablespoons powdered sugar
Lemon wedges, for squeezing

1   **Make the batter:** In a medium bowl, whisk together the flour, sugar, and salt. In a separate medium bowl, whisk the eggs.

2   In a small saucepan, combine the milk and butter over medium-low heat. Once the butter melts, remove from the heat—the mixture should be no warmer than body temperature. Pour it into the bowl with the beaten eggs and whisk together.

3   Pour the egg/milk mixture into the flour bowl and whisk until smooth, no more than a minute. Pour the batter through a fine-mesh sieve[1] into a bowl and set aside. Let the batter rest for at least 1 hour and up to 12 hours.

4   **Make the fillings:** In a small bowl, mix together the cream cheese, egg yolk, sugar, and salt to combine. Fold in the cottage cheese. In a separate bowl, mix together the guava jam and lemon juice. Set both bowls aside.

5   **Cook and assemble the blintzes:** In an 8-inch nonstick pan, melt a smidge of the butter over medium heat, and using a paper towel, wipe out any excess—it should be the lightest coating possible. Pour just shy of ⅓ cup of the batter into the pan, immediately swirling to coat the entire bottom in a thin layer. As soon as it looks set enough to flip, about 10 seconds, use the edge of a silicone spatula to help you pick up the blintz, flip it over, and cook for another 10 seconds. Flip out onto a plate. Repeat with the rest of the batter, adding butter and batter to the pan the same way each time, and stacking the finished blintzes on top of one another.

6   To fill each blintz, spoon 2 heaping tablespoons of the cheese mixture about 1 inch up from the bottom edge and spread it in a thick horizontal line across the blintz. Top the cheese mixture with about 2 teaspoons jam, spreading evenly. Fold the bottom up over the filling, then fold the left and right sides in. Roll the blintz away from you over the filling to create a filled cylindrical parcel. Repeat until you've stuffed all of the blintzes.

1
Straining makes sure you have a lump-free batter.

7 Preheat the oven to 350°F. Line a baking sheet with parchment paper.

8 Return the nonstick pan to medium heat and add a pat of the butter. Working in batches, add blintzes to the pan, seam-side down, and cook until lightly browned on the first side, 3 to 5 minutes, then flip and cook another 2 minutes to lightly brown the second side. Transfer the blintzes to the lined baking sheet, seam-side down.

9 Bake the blintzes until they heat all the way through, 7 to 8 minutes.

10 Serve them dusted with the powdered sugar. Garnish with lemon wedges.

Smoky Freekeh Fritters

Freekeh, if you're unfamiliar with it, is smoky green wheat berries, and you're going to flip for its sneaky charm. It's got all of the comforting qualities of bulgur but with more complex flavor and chewier texture. Here, it's coming in hot as a rice alternative in these cheesy, arancini-esque fritters. We highly recommend having a stash of these in the freezer, ready to fry at a moment's notice, and serving them with a little labneh (page 98) and Green Zhoug (page 95).

> Get Ahead
>
> You can prep everything well in advance but, as a rule to live by, always fry right before serving.

4 cups diced yellow onions (about 2 onions)

3 tablespoons unsalted butter

1 tablespoon plus 2 teaspoons kosher salt

½ teaspoon freshly ground black pepper

1 tablespoon plus 1 teaspoon ground fennel

1 bay leaf

1½ cups freekeh

4 ounces smoky cheese (such as smoked mozzarella or Gouda), grated

4 ounces melty, funky cheese (such as kashkaval, Gruyère, or Taleggio), grated

2 cups all-purpose flour

6 large eggs, beaten

4 cups panko bread crumbs

4 to 6 cups neutral oil, such as canola or sunflower

1. In a large pot, combine the onions, butter, salt, black pepper, ground fennel, and bay leaf and cook over medium heat, stirring occasionally, until the onions are soft, about 20 minutes.

2. Add the freekeh and 10 cups water.[1] Increase the heat to high and bring to a boil. Reduce to a simmer and cook until the water has fully absorbed and the freekeh resembles a very thick porridge, 2½ to 3 hours.[2] Stir occasionally at first, then frequently, scraping the bottom of the pot, as it thickens.

3. Once thickened, add the cheeses and stir to melt them in. Continue to reduce if the mixture is soupy—it should be thick! Once there, spread the mixture onto a baking sheet and let cool to room temperature. Transfer to the fridge to chill, at least 4 hours.

4. Line a baking sheet with parchment. Using a tablespoon, scoop the mixture into about 1½-inch balls, using your hands to roll,[3] and place on the prepared sheet. Freeze the balls on the tray, at least 2 hours or up to 12 hours.

5. Set up three medium bowls: Place the flour in one, the beaten eggs in a second, and the panko in the third. Working in batches, drop the balls into the flour, shaking off any excess. Then, pop them into the egg to coat, draining any excess using a slotted spoon. Next, roll them in the panko to evenly cover. Transfer them to a baking sheet and refrigerate until ready to fry. (If making ahead, you can freeze them at this point.)

6. Pour 2 to 3 inches of the oil into a deep heavy-bottomed pot over medium heat. Heat to 350°F then reduce the heat to medium-low.

7. Working in batches, fry until golden, 5 to 7 minutes (8 to 9 minutes if frozen).

1
You can add the water all at once; or, if your pot is on the smaller side, add it in stages à la risotto.

2
If the water has reduced down but the grains are still chewy, add another cup of water and keep cooking. We're looking for soft, porridgy grains here.

3
Have a little dish of water handy. If your hands get sticky while shaping, dabbing them with a little water helps to move things along.

Sweet Treats

Our dessert vibe is one of two things: very casual, like our Tahini Chocolate Chip Cookies (page 244), or a bit of an event. We're giving you mostly the latter here, thanks in large part to Meadow Ramsey, Kismet's longtime (and, in fact, all-time) pastry chef. Meadow is an incredible collaborator and a massive talent in her own right. (The Ricotta Cheesecake with Passion Fruit Caramel on page 256, for example, is 100 percent hers from start to finish.) Kismet would be a much less delicious place without her contributions, and we're thrilled to share a slice of that with you here.

Tahini Chocolate Chip Cookies

We've served scores of these at Kismet Rotisserie: They strike that archetypal balance of crispy edges and chewy center that we can all agree is *the* textural gold-standard for chocolate chip cookies. The tahini plays an important role, tempering the sweetness with a balancing bitter edge, a crucial detail for a not-too-sweet treat.

Get Ahead

If you want to make the cookie dough balls and freeze them for when a cookie moment calls, have at it. Just thaw them, uncovered, on a tray in the fridge for a few hours (or overnight) before baking.

1¾ cups all-purpose flour

1 teaspoon baking soda, sifted

1½ sticks (6 ounces) unsalted butter, at room temperature

¾ cup granulated sugar

¾ cup loosely packed dark brown sugar

1½ teaspoons kosher salt

¾ cup tahini

1 teaspoon vanilla extract

2 large eggs

2 cups roughly chopped dark chocolate (70% cacao[1])

1 tablespoon flaky sea salt

1 In a medium bowl, whisk together the flour and baking soda. Set aside.

2 In a stand mixer fitted with the paddle, cream together the butter, granulated sugar, brown sugar, and salt on medium speed until fluffy and light in color, about 10 minutes, stopping occasionally to scrape the sides and bottom of the bowl.

3 Turn the mixer off and add the tahini and vanilla. Mix on low speed to incorporate, then add the eggs, one at a time. Incorporate each fully, scraping down the bowl as needed.

4 Turn off the mixer and add the flour mixture to the bowl. On low speed, mix until almost fully combined, then add the chocolate and mix just to distribute. Transfer to the fridge, covered, for at least 2 hours or up to 12 hours.

5 Preheat the oven to 350°F. Line two baking sheets with parchment paper.

6 Scoop heaping tablespoons of dough into loose balls of roughly equal size—no need to roll them—and evenly space them 3 inches apart on each lined pan.

7 Top each cookie with a pinch of flaky salt and bake until browned on the edges but not all the way through, 12 to 14 minutes. Let cool and enjoy.

[1]

We recommend 70% chocolate, which offsets the sweetness of the cookie. You can use chocolate chips, if you prefer. Chopped chocolate yields a more fudgy, layered end result like you see in most bakeries these days, versus chips, which yield a more classic, studded, homey-looking cookie.

1
It helps to give it a mix by hand before turning the machine back on to avoid (even on low speed) having the flour mushroom-cloud out of the mixer. Just remove the paddle attachment and use it as you would a rubber spatula to mix a bit, then snap it back on and turn the mixer on to mix fully.

2
Baking from frozen is key in maintaining the round shape – a less frozen cookie will yield a flatter cookie. Once frozen, the dough balls can be transferred to an airtight container or resealable bag and returned to the freezer to have on hand anytime you want to bake off a few.

3
Rubbing the kosher salt between your fingers grinds it a little finer, therefore more evenly distributing it into the powdered sugar.

A Good Gluten-Free Cookie

MAKES ABOUT 36 COOKIES

Everyone needs at least one back-pocket dietary-restriction sweet in their repertoire. These more-or-less traditional wedding cookies are the ideal recipe to make gluten-free, because they are meant to have that classic crumbly crumb. Texturally, they're very satisfying, if a bit precarious. They shatter into an explosion of fine powder the second you bite into them—they should probably come with a warning. And don't even think about trying to talk while eating one of these bad boys: impossible. We suggest you enjoy the moment of silence and reflect upon how delightfully happy a small cinnamony snowball has just made you.

> **Get Ahead**
> The baked cookies will hold for up to 1 week in an airtight container.

2 sticks (8 ounces) unsalted butter, at room temperature

2½ cups powdered sugar

1¼ teaspoons kosher salt

½ teaspoon vanilla extract

2¼ cups gluten-free flour (we like Bob's Red Mill)

1¼ cups pecans, finely ground in a food processor

3 teaspoons ground cinnamon

1 In a stand mixer fitted with the paddle, combine the butter, ½ cup of the powdered sugar, ¾ teaspoon of the salt, and the vanilla and beat together, starting on low speed, then increasing to medium, until light and fluffy, 5 to 6 minutes, stopping to scrape the sides and bottom once or twice.

2 In a medium bowl, combine the flour, pecans, and 2 teaspoons of the cinnamon and whisk together.

3 Once the butter is creamed, stop the mixer and add the flour/pecan mixture.[1] On the lowest speed, mix to just combine, 20 to 30 seconds. Transfer to a covered bowl and refrigerate for at least 4 hours or up to 12 hours.

4 Remove the dough from the fridge and let it sit for 1 hour to soften a bit.

5 Line a baking sheet with parchment paper. Portion the dough into balls using a flat tablespoon measure, then roll each portion into small balls. Place on the lined baking sheet and freeze,[2] uncovered, for at least 4 hours.

6 Preheat the oven to 300°F. Line a second baking sheet with parchment paper and divide the frozen dough balls between the two baking sheets, spaced 2 inches apart.

7 Bake until they puff up and no longer look raw, 30 to 35 minutes.

8 In a medium bowl, combine the remaining 2 cups powdered sugar and 1 teaspoon cinnamon. Sprinkle in[3] the remaining ½ teaspoon salt. Whisk everything together. Transfer half to a wide shallow bowl.

9 Remove the cookies from the oven and let cool for 5 minutes. (The cookies will be very delicate at this point, but the sugar will stick to them best while still hot.) Using a spatula or your fingers, carefully relocate a few cookies at a time into the sugar mixture in the wide shallow bowl. Carefully spoon the reserved sugar over each cookie to fully coat. Transfer to a wire rack to cool. Repeat with the remaining cookies and let cool fully.

Sesame Buckwheat Blondies

This recipe began with our dear friend, the ultra-talented Pam Yung, who made the first version for the Glasserie menu in 2013, and we have her to thank for these buckwheat butter babies. Since then, these blondies have seen many iterations. Meadow, Kismet's pastry chef, has tweaked the recipe over the years and created a helpful shortcut: Make the batter in the pot you brown your butter in—genius.

They're a top-notch bake sale treat (they happen to be gluten-free), and they thrive alongside a scoop of vanilla ice cream. Word to the wise: Watch the bake time closely. The toasty, nutty, tip-top deliciousness of these blondies really shines when you bake them to a fudgy finish. Go too far, and you'll end up with cake.

½ cup sesame seeds
2 sticks (8 ounces) plus 1 tablespoon unsalted butter, plus more for greasing the pan
1¾ cups sugar
1 teaspoon kosher salt
3 large eggs
1¼ cups buckwheat flour
½ teaspoon baking powder

1 Preheat the oven to 325°F. Line a 9 × 13-inch quarter-baking sheet with parchment paper.

2 Spread the sesame seeds onto the pan and toast for 30 minutes, until lightly fragrant but not burnt. Remove from the oven.

3 Leave the oven on and reduce the temperature to 300°F.

4 When the parchment paper under the sesame seeds is cool enough to handle, lift it up and use it as a funnel to transfer the sesame seeds to a small bowl. Set aside. Grease the baking sheet (with a little oil or butter) and smooth the parchment paper back onto the pan.

5 In a large pot, melt the butter over medium-low heat and cook until it browns, 10 to 12 minutes. Remove the pot from the heat and let cool for 10 minutes—the butter should still be liquid.

6 Using a wooden spoon, stir the sugar and salt into the butter in the pot. Then add the eggs one at a time, stirring well after each addition until the mixture is smooth. Add the buckwheat flour and baking powder and stir until incorporated—the batter should look smooth.

7 Pour into the prepared baking sheet, scraping out any excess, and top evenly with the toasted sesame seeds. Bake until slightly puffy and a toothpick inserted in the center comes out clean, about 35 minutes.

8 Once cooled, cut into 12 squares.

Tropical Pudding Cups

Why do bananas get to have all the pudding fun? For a fresh perspective, we've taken a ginger-kissed pudding on a tropical vacation, mixing in kiwi, mango, papaya, and raspberries. We went with some easy-to-find fruits, but go wild! If you can locate any lychees, rambutans, mamey, sapotes, durian, or, hey, even bananas, we're out here cheering you on. For a nice extra touch, layer some gingersnaps (as you would Nilla wafers in a banana pudding) into the cups along with the fruit.

Get Ahead
The pudding can hold for up to 5 days, covered, in the fridge. Add the fruit when ready to serve.

1 large egg yolk
1 teaspoon vanilla extract
3 cups whole milk
¼ cup cornstarch
⅔ cup whole-milk powder[1]
½ cup sugar
⅛ teaspoon kosher salt
1-inch piece ginger, sliced
1 tablespoon unsalted butter
2 kiwis, peeled and chopped
½ mango, peeled and chopped
¼ papaya, peeled, seeded, and chopped
1 cup raspberries

1   Set a fine-mesh sieve over a heatproof medium bowl. In a second heatproof medium bowl, combine the egg yolk and vanilla, but wait to whisk together. Set both aside.

2   In a liquid measuring cup, whisk together ½ cup of the milk and the cornstarch to fully combine and set aside. (Be sure to rewhisk when ready to use, as the starch settles.)

3   In a medium saucepan, combine the remaining 2½ cups milk, the milk powder, sugar, salt, and ginger. Bring up to a light simmer over medium-high heat, stirring constantly with a silicone spatula, about 5 minutes. Reduce the heat to medium-low and continue stirring for another 15 minutes. Using a slotted spoon, remove the ginger from the pan.

4   Stream the milk/cornstarch mixture into the saucepan, stirring constantly, until fully incorporated. Cook over medium-low heat, stirring constantly, until the whole mixture starts to thicken, being careful not to scorch the bottom. When the consistency resembles pudding texture, remove it from the heat.

5   Whisk the egg yolk and vanilla together now. Then, adding about 1 tablespoon at a time, whisk about 1 cup of the hot pudding mixture into the egg yolk, continuing to whisk, to warm it (being careful not to cook the yolk). Return the contents of the bowl to the pan, stir thoroughly, and return to low heat for 15 to 30 seconds longer. Remove it from the heat and stir in the butter to fully incorporate.

6   Pour the pudding through the sieve set over the bowl, using your rubber spatula to help push it through, working in batches if needed. Place plastic wrap directly onto the surface of the pudding, covering it completely, and transfer to the fridge until fully chilled, at least 4 hours or up to several days.

7   When ready to assemble, whisk the pudding vigorously to smooth it out. Toss the cut fruit together in a bowl. Alternating pudding and fruit, layer into (ideally glass) serving dishes.

[1]
You should be able to easily find milk powder in any grocery store in the baking section.

Roasted Peaches + Almond Cream

Peaches and cream is *the* treat for hot summer days. Roasting your peaches is the swanky step up you never knew you needed. Think of this version as the classic's older sister, all grown up: She's got air conditioning, has no problem turning on the stove when the temps outside hit 90, and likes to impress. Juxtaposed with cold, almond-laced cream, the season's best fruit finds a winning partner. Added bonus: Roasting gives subpar fruit a little lift, but perfect peaches are always welcome.

Get Ahead

Steep the toasted almonds in cream a day, or several, before to get a head start. Toast your almonds the second time and you've got your cream and almonds waiting in the wings for whenever your peaches come out of the oven. With the steps spread out over time like that, this recipe will feel like no work at all.

¼ cup sliced almonds

½ cup heavy cream

Pinch of kosher salt

2 tablespoons sugar

Grated zest of ½ lemon

1 tablespoon lemon juice (about ½ lemon)

2 peaches, halved and pitted

1 tablespoon unsalted butter,
    cut into small pieces

1 Preheat the oven to 300°F.

2 Spread the almonds on a baking sheet and toast until lightly browned, about 15 minutes. Let cool.

3 In a small saucepan, gently warm the cream over low heat until just steaming, about 10 minutes. Transfer the cream to a sealable heatproof container and stir in the cooled almonds. Transfer to the fridge and let steep for at least 4 hours.

4 Preheat the oven to 275°F. Line a baking sheet with parchment paper.

5 Pour the almond/cream mixture through a fine-mesh sieve set over a small bowl. Press as much liquid as you can out of the almonds in the sieve, then transfer the almonds to a small bowl. Return the almond cream to the fridge.

6 Toss the almonds with the salt and 1 tablespoon of the sugar. Spread them out into a flat layer on the lined baking sheet. Bake until golden brown, about 1½ hours. Let cool completely before storing in an airtight container.

7 Increase the oven temperature to 350°F.

8 In a small bowl, stir together the lemon zest, lemon juice, and remaining 1 tablespoon sugar. Set the peaches cut-side up into a small baking dish. Spoon the lemony sugar over the peaches and dot each one with butter.

9 Roast the peaches until jammy, about 50 minutes.

10 Place a warm peach half in each bowl. Divide the cold almond cream among the four bowls, pouring it over the peaches. Sprinkle each with toasted almonds.

Labneh Panna Cotta
with Strawberries

Panna cotta is a creamy, all-seasons crowd-pleaser, but the real reason you see it on so many restaurant menus is that it's just really *really* easy. Make it early in the day and, come evening, you've got a very satisfying, effortlessly impressive dessert ready and waiting for you. We give the classic panna a microdose of sophistication, via tangy labneh and rose water–scented strawberries.

Panna Cotta
½ cup labneh, store-bought or homemade (page 98)
1 teaspoon vanilla extract
1½ teaspoons unflavored gelatin powder
1 cup buttermilk, cold
2 cups heavy cream
½ cup sugar
¼ teaspoon kosher salt

Strawberries
1 pint strawberries, sliced
¼ cup sugar
Pinch of kosher salt
1 teaspoon red wine vinegar
¼ teaspoon rose water

1 **Make the panna cotta:** In a medium bowl, combine the labneh and vanilla.

2 In a small bowl, sprinkle the gelatin over the buttermilk and let sit for 5 minutes. Once the gelatin has softened, whisk the buttermilk mixture into the labneh.

3 In a small saucepan, combine the heavy cream, sugar, and salt and warm over medium heat until just steaming—stir frequently and don't let it boil. Whisk the warm cream into the labneh mixture to combine. Pour the mixture through a fine-mesh sieve into a small pitcher or spouted measuring cup.

4 Pour the panna cotta into six individual 8-ounce cups and carefully transfer them to the fridge, uncovered, for at least 6 hours, until the panna cotta is fully set.

5 **Macerate the strawberries:** In a bowl, gently toss together the sliced strawberries, sugar, salt, vinegar, and rose water. Let sit for 5 to 10 minutes for the sugar to dissolve.

6 Just before serving, top the panna cottas with the strawberries.

Ricotta Cheesecake
with Passion Fruit Caramel

This cheesecake might just achieve food-of-the-gods status, no surprise to anyone who knows Kismet's longtime pastry chef, Meadow Ramsey, whose talent is worthy of such a title. With the addition of passion fruit caramel—inspired by Meadow's time working under the legendary Claudia Fleming at Gramercy Tavern—the cake's richness is cut by a welcome hit of acidity. That said, it's not the simplest recipe, and attention must be paid any time one bakes using a water bath. However, this technique is what makes the texture creamy and dense yet somehow also paradoxically light.

To help you achieve water bath success, make sure you use boiling water. Always add the water to the pan once it's already in the oven, with the door open. When you're pulling the baked cheesecake out, you'll want to first lift the cheesecake pan from the water. Never move the water pan with the cheesecake in it or you'll risk a dessert-destroying tsunami. If you pull it off (and you will), your care will be rewarded with a truly impressive sweet treat.

See photo on page 242.

Get Ahead
The caramel holds for 2 weeks in the fridge—just hold off on mixing in the fresh passion fruit pulp until the day you're serving it.

The cheesecake itself can be made up to 3 days ahead.

Crust

6 tablespoons unsalted butter
1½ cups graham cracker crumbs
(10 to 12 full cracker sheets)
½ cup loosely packed dark brown sugar
¾ teaspoon kosher salt

1 Preheat the oven to 300°F.

2 **Make the crust:** In a small saucepan, melt the butter over low heat. Remove the pan from the heat.

3 In a food processor, pulverize the graham crackers to fine crumbs. (Alternatively, crush them in a sealed bag, using a rolling pin.) Transfer the crumbs to a medium bowl and stir in the brown sugar and salt. Pour in the melted butter and stir thoroughly to combine. Transfer the graham-cracker mixture to a 9-inch springform pan and press down across the bottom using a flat object, such as the bottom of a measuring cup, to flatten the crust evenly.

4 Bake the crust for 15 minutes to set, then let cool for 30 minutes.

5 Cut 4 sheets of foil about 18 inches in length, and stack them on top of one another, crisscrossing each sheet. On top of the foil, repeat the same pattern with 4 sheets of plastic wrap.[1] Place the springform pan on top of the plastic and crimp the edges of the foil up the sides of the pan, tucking the plastic in underneath it, forming a barrier between the pan and the water bath it will sit in. (Alternatively, if you have a 10-inch silicone or metal cake pan, you can set the 9-inch springform inside of that.)

1
We wouldn't advise you to put plastic in the oven if it was sitting directly on your food, but it is an essential barrier here, making sure the water doesn't leak into your cheesecake. There are good silicone options to use instead of foil/plastic, if you want to explore an alternative.

2
Use store-bought labneh instead of our homemade labneh, which is too thin for the cheesecake.

3
Passion fruit puree is sold frozen and often as a cocktail mixer. If your grocery store doesn't stock it, try a specialty bar, baking supply shop, or the internet.

Cheesecake Filling

½ vanilla bean (optional), split lengthwise

1 pound cream cheese, at room temperature

¾ cup sugar

½ teaspoon kosher salt

1 cup ricotta cheese

1 cup store-bought labneh[2]

2 teaspoons vanilla extract

3 large eggs

Caramel

¾ cup sugar

½ teaspoon kosher salt

1 tablespoon light corn syrup

3 tablespoons unsalted butter,
     at room temperature

⅓ cup passion fruit puree,[3] thawed

1 passion fruit (optional), contents stirred

6   In a medium pot or a kettle, bring 8 to 12 cups of water to a boil.

7   **Make the cheesecake filling:** If using the vanilla bean, scrape the seeds into the bowl of a stand mixer fitted with the paddle. Add the cream cheese, sugar, and salt and beat on low speed until smooth, about 2 minutes. Scrape down the sides, increase the speed to medium, and beat until fluffy, 4 to 5 minutes. Add the ricotta, labneh, and vanilla extract and beat on low speed to combine. Add the eggs, one at a time, beating well on low speed after each addition and scraping down the sides before moving on to the next. When all of the eggs are incorporated, pour the filling into the prepared crust pan.

8   Place the springform pan, within its barrier, into a large baking dish or roasting pan—about 12 × 16 inches—the springform should sit completely flat. Transfer to the oven (don't pull the rack out) and, with the oven door open, carefully pour boiling water into the baking dish. It should be filled to about halfway up the sides of the pan, so add only as much as you need.

9   Bake until the sides puff up but the center still wobbles, 45 minutes to 1 hour, very carefully rotating once halfway through.

10   Again, without pulling the rack out, carefully lift the springform pan from the water bath and set on a wire rack to cool to room temp, about 1½ hours. Transfer to the fridge to set for at least 6 hours. (When the baking dish/roasting pan that was left in the oven is cool enough to safely handle, remove it and discard the water.)

11   **Make the caramel:** In a small saucepan, combine the sugar, salt, and corn syrup and heat over medium heat. Pour 3 tablespoons water down the sides of the pan into the sugar mixture and, using a heat-resistant silicone spatula, incorporate carefully and fully from the edge inward. Cook, undisturbed, for 5 minutes. The mixture should be clear in color and furiously bubbling. Keeping a close eye, when the color begins to change, carefully swirl the caramel as it darkens. When the color is medium golden all the way through, remove from the heat and quickly whisk in the soft butter until fully incorporated. Pour the passion fruit puree into the caramel and allow to sit for 30 seconds before whisking to smooth. Cool completely at room temp. If using, stir in the fresh passion fruit pulp and seeds.

12   When ready to serve, remove the springform band and top the cheesecake with passion fruit caramel, either over the whole cake or spooned onto individual slices. Cut the cheesecake by dipping a knife into hot water and wiping it dry between cutting the slices.

Creamsicle Cake

Day or night, this (incidentally gluten-free) layered lady makes the perfect light-n-citrusy celebration cake. The key to getting the airy, not-a-care-in-the-world texture right is not to overwhip the egg whites (or the cream)—pay a little extra attention to your mixer. That said, as it's soaked (a la tres leches), it's very forgiving.

When picking out your oranges, you want fruit with some no-joke acidity to cut through the cream. Look to sharper varieties like mandarins and blood oranges in addition to mellow options like navels and Cara Caras. Citrus is nicest in winter, so to make this cake for a summer soiree, a lovely alt version could sub in raspberries for citrus and rose water for orange blossom.

See photo on page 260.

Get Ahead
You can assemble this cake up to a day ahead of time, but note that you'll want to keep it covered if you're holding it for more than a couple hours in the fridge. For presentation's sake, hold off on the final layer of oranges until the cake no longer needs to be covered.

Cooking spray, oil, or butter, for the
   baking sheet

Cake
2⅔ cups almond flour
¼ cup cornstarch
2 teaspoons baking powder
12 large eggs, separated
1⅓ cups sugar
⅛ teaspoon kosher salt
Grated zest of 1 orange

Oranges
3 cups diced oranges
½ cup orange marmalade
¼ teaspoon kosher salt
2 tablespoons lemon juice (about 1 lemon)

Milk Soak
3 cups whole milk
1 cup orange marmalade
¼ teaspoon kosher salt

Whipped Cream
4 cups heavy cream
2 tablespoons sugar
2 teaspoons orange blossom water

1. Preheat the oven to 325°F. Grease the bottom of a 13 × 18-inch baking sheet with cooking spray or a small amount of oil or butter. Line the bottom of the pan with parchment paper. Set aside.

2. **Make the cake:** Line a baking sheet with parchment paper. Spread the almond flour onto it and toast in the oven until lightly golden brown, about 30 minutes, stirring once or twice for even color. Let cool to room temperature, about 20 minutes.

3. Leave the oven on.

4. Using the parchment paper as a funnel, transfer the toasted almond flour to a medium bowl. Whisk in the cornstarch and baking powder and set aside.

5. In a stand mixer fitted with the whisk, combine the egg whites, ⅔ cup of the sugar, and the salt. Mix on medium-high speed to form glossy peaks, 3 to 4 minutes.[1] Transfer the whites to a separate large bowl.

6. Rinse and dry the mixer bowl and whisk. Set back on the mixer and add the egg yolks, remaining ⅔ cup sugar, and the orange zest. Whisk on medium-high until light and ribbony, about 3 minutes.

1
If you're whisking by hand or with a handheld mixer, it's going to take you much longer, but don't give up!

2
Alternatively, you can use the back side of another baking sheet if you don't have a large cutting board.

3
Choose a dish that the cake can sit flat on but that has a lip and a little room to catch the milk soak. Ideally, a wide and shallow dish with a flat bottom or a rectangular baking dish would work as well.

7   Using a rubber spatula, working in three equal batches, gently fold the egg whites into the yolks to combine. Then, in two batches, fold in the almond flour mixture to fully incorporate. Spread the batter evenly onto the prepared baking sheet.

8   Bake until fully set and the top is golden brown, about 50 minutes, rotating the pan front to back halfway through. Let cool to room temp in the pan, at least 45 minutes.

9   **Prep the oranges:** In a bowl, mix together the oranges, marmalade, salt, and lemon juice and set aside.

10   **Make the milk soak:** In a liquid measuring cup (or any container with a spout), whisk together the milk, marmalade, and salt. Set aside.

11   **Whip the cream:** In a stand mixer fitted with the whisk, combine the cream, sugar, and orange blossom water and whip on medium speed just until stiff peaks form, being careful not to overwhip.

12   To assemble the cake, use a knife to loosen the cake from the sides of the pan. Place a cutting board larger than the size of the baking sheet[2] gently onto the cake and, holding the pan against it, flip the cake out onto the cutting board. Peel off the parchment paper and trim the edges of the cake to make them even. Cut the cake in half crosswise into two identical 9 × 13-inch rectangles.

13   Place one cake layer, bottom-side up, onto a serving dish.[3] Gently pour half of the milk soak evenly over the cake. Spread two-thirds of the oranges with their liquid evenly over the top of the cake, followed by half the whipped cream, spreading evenly over the oranges. Place the other cake layer, bottom-side up, on top of the whipped cream. Soak the second layer with the rest of the milk soak.

14   Transfer to the fridge, along with the remaining whipped cream and oranges, and let sit for at least 1 hour uncovered (and up to overnight if you can cover it without ruining it) before serving.

15   To finish, spread the rest of the whipped cream evenly over the top of the cake and decorate with the remaining oranges.

Blueberry-Maple Sufganiot

Sufganiot, or jelly doughnuts, are the quintessential Chanukah sweet. These are an oil-themed (key for Chanukah) treat for those particular eight days of the year, but we can all agree that doughnuts don't need a holiday to have a place at the table. These little poofs, fragrant from the buckwheat and stuffed with blueberry jam and maple cream (for an unconventional touch), are a celebration unto themselves.

Get Ahead

Make the maple cream ahead and store it in the fridge for up to 1 day. Rewhip it a bit if it's gone flabby.

If you want to hold off on frying the doughnuts after shaping them, you can pop them in the fridge to slow down the proofing for up to 6 hours. Just pull them out 30 or so minutes before you want to fry them.

Doughnuts

1¾ cups all-purpose flour,
    plus more for kneading
¼ cup buckwheat flour
Canola oil, for the bowl
⅔ cup whole milk
1 (¼-ounce) envelope active dry yeast
    (2¼ teaspoons)
4 tablespoons unsalted butter, melted
    and cooled to room temperature
1 large egg, whisked
⅓ cup sugar
⅛ teaspoon kosher salt

Maple Cream

½ cup heavy cream
2 tablespoons maple syrup
⅛ teaspoon kosher salt
½ cup mascarpone

To Finish

3 to 4 cups canola oil
1 cup blueberry jam
¼ cup powdered sugar

1   **Make the doughnuts:** In a small bowl, whisk together the all-purpose and buckwheat flours. Set aside.

2   Grease a medium bowl with a touch of canola oil and set aside.

3   In a small saucepan, gently warm the milk over medium-low heat for 1 to 1½ minutes. Transfer to a medium bowl, stir in the yeast, and let sit until foamy, 5 to 10 minutes.

4   Once foamy, mix in the melted butter, egg, sugar, and salt and stir to combine. Add the flour mixture and stir with a wooden spoon to bring it together.

5   Turn the dough out onto a lightly floured surface and knead for 5 minutes, using additional flour as needed, to develop a homogeneous, smooth dough. It should be a sticky dough, so add only as much additional flour as you need to keep it from sticking too much (no more than ¼ cup total). Transfer to the greased bowl, cover, and let rise until doubled in size, about 1½ hours.

6   Line a baking sheet with parchment paper.[1] Turn the dough out onto a lightly floured surface. Fold it over itself two or three times, then pat the dough down into a disk 1 inch thick. Use a 2½-inch round cutter or a glass to punch out rounds, dipping the cutter into flour as you go, and place the rounds on the lined baking sheet. Reroll the scraps together and punch out more, to yield about 12 total.

7   Cover the doughnuts loosely with plastic and let rise until doubled in size, 1 to 1½ hours depending on the ambient temperature. (Try to make sure the plastic is loose enough to allow the doughnuts to proof but that it's still protecting them against the air so they don't form a skin.)

1

To easily slip the doughnuts into the hot oil without deflating them, cut the parchment paper into individual squares, placing each doughnut onto its own square before proofing. Then pick each one up by its parchment and flip it into the oil, pulling the parchment away as you do.

8   **Make the maple cream:** In a stand mixer fitted with the whisk (or in a large bowl whisking by hand), combine the cream, maple syrup, and salt and whisk on medium-high speed until stiff peaks form, about 3 minutes.

9   Spoon the mascarpone into a medium bowl and use a rubber spatula to fold the whipped cream into it until the mixture is homogeneous. Hand-whip with a whisk for 15 to 20 seconds to form a stiff cream. Set aside in the fridge.

10 **To finish:** When the doughnuts have risen, pour 2 inches of oil into a heavy-bottomed medium pot and heat to 350°F. Line a tray or large plate with paper towels.

11 Working in batches, being careful not to overcrowd the pot, fry the doughnuts until puffy and medium-brown, about 45 seconds per side (1½ to 2 minutes each). Remove them from the oil with a slotted spoon and transfer to the paper towels to drain.

12 Let the doughnuts cool for 15 minutes, then use a serrated knife to cut each doughnut in half horizontally. Spoon about 1 tablespoon each of jam and maple cream onto the bottom half and cap with the top half. Using a fine-mesh sieve, dust them with powdered sugar and serve immediately.

Milk Chocolate Tart

This tart tastes like a fancy candy bar, and that's kinda the idea. We channel a little childhood joy by using mostly milk chocolate (hello, old friend), while dark chocolate and nutty tahini keep the tart from tasting too cloying. We think it will please the adult and the kid in all of us.

Get Ahead

You can make all of the components in advance and combine them whenever you like. The chocolate mix can be made a week or two ahead and reheated over a double boiler or in a microwave. The tart shell holds in the freezer, unbaked and wrapped, for 2 to 3 months. The sesame whip holds for a day or two — you can always rewhip it to perk it up.

Tart Shell

¾ cup all-purpose flour,
     plus more for dusting
¼ cup semolina flour
¼ cup sugar
¼ teaspoon kosher salt
Grated zest of ½ lemon
1 large egg, cold
1 teaspoon heavy cream
1 teaspoon olive oil
4 tablespoons unsalted butter,
     cubed and cold

Filling

1½ cups chopped milk chocolate
½ cup chopped dark chocolate (70% cacao)
¼ teaspoon kosher salt
½ cup tahini
½ teaspoon vanilla extract
½ teaspoon toasted sesame oil
1½ cups heavy cream

Sesame Whip

1½ cups heavy cream
3 tablespoons sugar
¼ teaspoon toasted sesame oil
⅛ teaspoon kosher salt

1 **Make the tart shell:** In a stand mixer fitted with the paddle, combine the all-purpose flour, semolina flour, sugar, salt, and lemon zest. Beat together on low speed to combine.

2 In a glass measuring cup, whisk together the egg, cream, olive oil, and 1 teaspoon cold water. Set aside.

3 Add the cubed butter to the flour mixture in the mixer and mix on low speed until the mixture comes together into pea-size pieces. Slowly stream in the egg/cream mixture[1] and mix until the dough comes together into a ball, being careful not to overmix — it should be a smooth, homogeneous dough. Pat the dough into a disk and wrap it tightly in plastic. Refrigerate for at least 2 hours and up to 24 hours.

4 When ready to roll, generously dust a piece of parchment paper with all-purpose flour. Roll the dough into an even round ¼ inch thick, continuing to lift and dust with more flour to avoid sticking, until the entire round is 11 to 12 inches in diameter. Carefully lift the dough[2] into a 9-inch tart pan and press into the pan, fitting the dough snugly into the edges and against the fluted rim. Trim any excess at the top to a flat edge. Transfer the tart pan to the freezer for at least 1 hour.

5 Preheat the oven to 325°F.

6 Line the frozen tart shell with a piece of parchment[3] and fill with pie weights or baking beans (you can use any dried beans or even rice here). Bake for 20 minutes, rotating the pan front to back halfway through. Carefully remove the parchment, being careful to lift out the baking beans without spilling them, and return the pan to the oven to bake until golden and crisp, another 15 minutes. Let cool fully.

1
You may not need all of the liquid — err on the side of caution, because a too-wet dough is tricky to work with.

2
If your dough has warmed up quite a bit while rolling it out, it'll be difficult to work with. You may want to transfer it (on a baking sheet) into the fridge for 5 to 10 minutes to cool. On the flip side, if it's too cold, it will be brittle and break when trying to fit it into the tart pan — it's a real Goldilocks sitch.

3
Crumpling the parchment and smoothing it back out before fitting it into the frozen tart shell is a nifty trick, making it easier to fit into the nooks than a flat fresh piece.

7 **Make the filling:** In a heatproof medium bowl, combine the milk chocolate, dark chocolate, salt, tahini, vanilla, and sesame oil. In a small saucepan over low heat, warm the cream to the point of just starting to steam, about 5 minutes. Pour the hot cream into the bowl with the chocolate mixture and let sit for 2 minutes to melt, then whisk to smooth. Pour the chocolate mixture into the cooled tart shell and transfer to the fridge until fully set, 3 to 4 hours.

8 **Make the sesame whip:** In a medium bowl (or in a stand mixer with the whisk), whisk the cream, sugar, sesame oil, and salt to soft peaks.

9 Cut the tart into 8 wedges and top each with a dollop of sesame whip cream.

Acknowledgments

Even more overwhelming than writing this book is summing up the immense gratitude we feel for all of the people in our lives who have helped and been there for us. The contents of these pages contain so many years of work and growth, and so many people have influenced us over the years. It's hard to put it all into words, but here's an insufficient attempt!

We've dedicated this book to them, but it goes without saying that our parents, Debbie, Bruce, Eva, and Jerry, have always given us unflinching encouragement in pursuing our careers. Our siblings, Daniel, Dana, and Jonathan, are constant supports in our lives as well. We love you all very much.

The teams at Kismet and at Kismet Rotisserie, both past and present, have been the lifeblood of our businesses. We'd be lost without you all, namely Chad Alligood, Meadow Ramsey, Erik Girton, Neal Winterbotham, June Lopez, Iliana Loza, Kelsey Gray, Anna Polacek, and Emma Newbern.

Our publisher, Clarkson Potter, and the whole impressive team that we've been lucky enough to collaborate with: our editors Francis Lam and Susan Roxborough, as well as Jana Branson, Stephanie Davis, and Darian Keels, and the design team, including Robert Diaz and Stephanie Huntwork, along with Patricia Shaw, Kim Tyner, and Chris Tanigawa.

Chris Bernabeo, what a pleasure it was to spend many hours with you—never once did it feel like work. Kalen Kaminski, your impeccable taste has made everything in this book look beyond beautiful.

Julia Kramer, you are indispensable, that's all we'll say.

Thank you to Claire Hungerford for your inspired contributions to the design and to the Kismet aesthetic generally.

Thank you to our partners at KarpReilly who made it possible for us to continue to pursue our vision for Kismet into the future.

A world of gratitude to the brilliant Lilli Sherman and her team at Oma for their insight and for always pointing us in the right direction.

So many thanks to our recipe testers and culinary assistants for the shoots, Oliver Erteman and Alex Berry. You two made photographing more than a hundred recipes in ten days possible. And thank you to Gaby Chiongbian-Gagnon and all of our beautiful friends who came out to pose for pictures.

To our recipe-tester friends, Kate Thomas, Challen Hodson, and Callie Barlow—thank you, your feedback was so so helpful.

Special thank-yous to Helen Levi, Fell Knives, Justin Caraco, Whitebark Workwear, Unearthen, Chez Diane, Fredericks and Mae, Our Place, and Sophie Lou Jacobsen, for your contributions!

Sarah Hymanson: Thank you to my friends (you know who you are) for keeping me centered, helping me to feel like myself, and truly bringing so much joy into my life. Thank you, Carmen, for wrapping my jar of tea in a towel, for making sure I don't leave the house wearing wrinkled clothes, for getting up early to water the garden, and for always being more than down to travel far to eat delicious food. You're the best.

Thank you to SK for being the most hard-working, determined, and thoughtful partner. Thank you for putting so much of yourself into this book. Thank you for always celebrating our successes. Thank you for always pushing me and for believing that anything is possible—because with you, it is.

Sara Kramer: I'm overcome with love for my friends in LA, NY, and beyond. Thank you for always letting me cook for you, for your enthusiasm, and for always making me feel loved. I'm so grateful to the broader food and restaurant community for welcoming me in, for giving me purpose, and for the endless humility.

Hymanson, you're the hardest-working person I've ever met. I'm thrilled every time you take a break, and even happier (and relieved) when you return. I'm lucky to know you and witness the breadth of your talent and hugeness of your heart at such a close distance. Thank you for always having patience for me and everyone and everything.

Index

Note: Page references in *italics* indicate photographs.